Apples of Gold in Settings of Silver

Apples of Gold in Settings of Silver

Deborah Louise Off

Apples of Gold in Settings of Silver

ISBN 979-8-9994855-0-2 paperback
ISBN 979-8-9994855-1-9 eBook

"A word aptly spoken is like
apples of gold in settings of silver."
—*Proverbs 25:11*

The title of my collection of writings is taken from this Bible verse. It tells of the power of our words. The words I write here tell the stories of my life.

But I also cherish *my* "apples of gold"—*the life and family* God has given to me; and *my* "settings of silver"—the *place* where my family and I live along the seashore of the southern New Jersey coast.

Deborah Louise Off

Lord, thank you for helping me write this journey of faith. I pray these stories will bring a bit of Your love, Your happiness, and especially Your wonder to every reader.

Lord, I dedicate Apples of Gold in Settings of Silver to You.

Contents

This Is Me

*T*here are two decisions I have made in my life that I have never regretted. Without them I am sure I would not be the person I am today. They are still the most important and best things I have ever done in my life.

The *most important thing* I did was to ask Jesus into my heart, to forgive all my wrongs, and to help me serve Him every day. I am not a Bible-quoting Christian evangelical. Though I admire those who do have the voice, or the guts, to do that, I am a quiet, shy girl. But God is the center of my life. I talk to Him all the time. I know Him, and He knows me. He accepts me just the way I am, which is good. I fail Him often, and then He corrects me in His gentle way. I know the peace He gives.

I believe in the God of the Passover and the God of Easter. I pray daily for guidance, wisdom, protection, and help. My father taught me to do that. Dad was a tall, strong man with broad shoulders, black wavy hair, blue eyes, and gentle ways. He was born in 1916. His father died when my dad was five. Dad was raised by his mother, then by two stepfathers he often talked about, and whom he loved dearly. (Yes, my grandmother was widowed three times.) Dad was put to the test in his life. He would say, "You ask God to take care of you and give you wisdom. He will give it to you. He knows." And I do. God always answers my prayers, sometimes fast, sometimes slow, sometimes *real* slow.

The *best thing* I ever did in my life was to marry my best friend, Bill Off. I was fifteen and he was nineteen when we started dating. I lived in Cheltenham, Pennsylvania, and he lived in Linwood, New Jersey, a town across the bay from Ocean City. We saw each other only on weekends and wrote to each other almost every day. We talked on the phone once a week when Bill would go to a phone booth near the Garden State Parkway with a roll of quarters and we would talk until the money was gone. I loved his quiet, fun ways, his soft voice, his blue, blue eyes, and his love for the Lord. We dated for three and a half years.

We were married on March 24, 1973, by his minister at my church, Berachah Church, in Cheltenham. We moved to the south end of Ocean City, and so began our life together. Bill worked at his family's business, a greenhouse range where they grew orchids. We had five beautiful children, three girls and two boys. I was a stay-at-home mom. We had our ups and downs, laughter and sadness. We never had a lot of money, but we had a lot of faith. We were happy.

Today, our children are grown, working, and have homes and families of their own. Bill owns the same orchid business and is the hardest working person I have ever met. I worked with Down syndrome and autistic children at the local high school for many years and at the same time challenged myself to get a college degree.

I write because I believe God wants me to do so; and who am I to say "No" to the author of the number one best seller?

Writing is hard. It is a grueling task to sit in front of a blank page and say, "Now what, Lord?" I am weak but willing. He is strong and powerful. We're a team, an undeniable force. I try and I fail; I trust, and I succeed.

My stories are a journey of faith and wonder that wind from the days of my childhood to now. They are stories of love, money, dogs, faith, family, work, simple things, even goofy things that have happened to me, and lessons I have learned; yes, even some lessons I learned the hard way. In a lot of my stories, you will hear me call on the Lord; in other stories, I hope you will see and feel God's love, and most of all, I hope you will feel His wonder.

My greatest desire is that my written voice will encourage and bring joy, even laughter, to people when they need it most.

An Autumn Day

I remember when I was eight years old, walking down the full two-block length of our street, Arbor Road, in Cheltenham, Pennsylvania. I was alone. It was a cold autumn day. The leaves were deep and scattered on the ground, and the tree branches were bare and gnarled against the gray sky.

I was not cold because I wore a red knit hat and a thick, red cardigan sweater. Far above my head, the wind blew, and the massive branches creaked back and forth seeming to scratch that cloudy sky. Leaves danced in the wind and rose from the ground in a flurry. Whether this was the first time I ventured so far from home—all two blocks—by myself, I do not know, but I do remember that I saw houses and I did not know who lived in them. However, I wasn't afraid. There was a quietness in the walk; just me, the leaves, the skeleton trees, and that gray windy sky. I don't remember turning around to go home, but I must have done so.

To this very day, I love to see a gray sky. Bare branches against that gray sky are still one of my favorites too. This recollection from my childhood, of such a peaceful time, always comes to my mind in the autumn. The rest of the year, this memory is buried deep in my thoughts, waiting to be called upon.

This is what writing is all about.

I like to think of myself not only as a writer but also as a storyteller. Just like that one fall day many years ago, my life now is quiet, happy, and peaceful. Suddenly, memories dormant for a long-time surface when I least expect them. Memories, sights, sounds, and feelings can trigger me to say, "Hey, I gotta write that down..."

Then the story is born.

I pen those rich remembrances of people, places, events, faith, and feelings onto paper; some are happy, some funny, some sad, and some profound. I have written these stories over many years; yet they still evoke timeless lessons and emotions in me. I do believe that the Lord wants me to share them. I have changed a few names to protect the innocent or the bashful; but of course, I do that with love for each of them.

It is okay to read this book a little at a time. There is no hurry to get to the end to see what happens. There is no end. There is only the *continuation of wonder.*

Yes, the best part of each story *is the wonder* . . . and that I leave to you, the reader.

Grandmom

I often wonder what I am going to be like when I get old. I have a list of things I have observed in older people I have known. I am not going to be a grouch; I will always play with children; and, I will always be a good cook, even if I cook for only me.

I would like to tell you about my father's mother, the only grandmother I ever knew. Her name was Carolyn Augusta Held. She was a small woman in height, maybe four foot eleven inches tall, and a large woman in breadth, weighing about two hundred pounds. She was always fat. As she told it, she didn't know she was fat until a woman sitting next to her on a bus asked her, "Why are you so fat?" I remember Grandmom could not believe the woman's nerve, though the lady was probably sharing a seat with Grandmom.

Grandmom had silver gray/white hair, always in a French knot at the back of her head. She used hair combs studded with rhinestones to keep the hair on the side of her head in place. My earliest Christmas memory of Grandmom was when she stayed overnight at our house on Christmas Eve. She slept with me in my room. Of course, I went to bed early. I remember my shock waking up the next morning with Grandmom next to me in my double bed. There was this large lady in a light blue cotton nightgown whom I thought I didn't know. Her hair was down, and it was long, very long, and gray. It hung down over her cheek and curled across her shoulder and down her back. Her mouth was open in sleep, and to my surprise, she had no teeth!

I got up some nerve and nudged her. "Grandmom," I said softly. "Grandmom," I said again. "It's Christmas!"

She opened her eyes, and all doubt went away when I saw those twinkling hazel green eyes. "Well, so it is," she said. "Merry Christmas, Debby!"

"Merry Christmas, Grandmom!" I scurried out of bed to get dressed. "Oh, my gosh, what's that?" I said, pointing to a plastic bowl on my dresser. It was filled with water and something that looked creepy.

Grandmom chuckled and said, "They're my 'teef'!"

Grandmom spent every Christmas Eve and Christmas Day with us that I can remember. She always wore a dress that buttoned down the front, usually flowered, and always with a rhinestone broach. She wore those black old-lady lace-up shoes with the two-inch square heel and what looked like a hole in front for her big toe. She never went out without a hat.

Grandmom had beautiful skin, rosy cheeks, and a hearty laugh. She had a slow walk, sort of side to side, as someone of her size would. She out-lived three husbands, but I never knew any of them. She had six children of her own and nine stepchildren.

Grandmom lived alone in a very small third-floor apartment above a bakery, on a noisy city street in Philadelphia. It had two rooms and a bathroom, and it was just plain old-fashioned. The kitchen had a one-piece porcelain sink and drainboard with silver hot-and-cold handles and separate spigots. Around the bottom of the sink was a green skirt that hid her trash can and paper bags. An old green and yellow gas stove stood on short legs near the sink. Large white, wooden cabinets with paned glass doors held her dishes. The kitchen table always had a bowl of fresh fruit on it, usually bananas.

In a small, white metal hutch she kept her dish towels and pots and pans. As a nosey little girl, I opened all the doors and drawers of that cabinet. One drawer held a small glass jar full of pennies. I remember the lid of the jar had the picture of a black bear on it, probably an old honey jar. In the opposite corner of the kitchen was a wringer washer, which usually had a cloth over it.

The refrigerator was small and usually had a saucer of used tea bags on the shelf to be used again (after all, she had lived through the Depression). The top of the refrigerator had a small pull-down door that was the freezer. Now I realize that, all those years, Grandmom's freezer was probably on the blink. Every Friday night we would go to her place and have Neapolitan ice cream that was as soft as mush. We would swirl it all together to make our own soft serve and drop broken pretzels in it. To this day, Neapolitan ice cream brings Grandmom to mind.

Grandmom's living room was also her bedroom. From outside the windows came the muffled sounds of buses and cars on the busy street below. In that room was a double bed, a rocking chair, two goose-neck rockers, a new hi-fidelity phonograph, a dresser, a vanity and small bench, a tall secretary desk, and a spooky wooden closet in the corner that was never open. And pictures: family pictures and paintings. Her second husband, Karl Huf, was an artist. He created the Campbell Soup kids—my aunt and uncle, when they were little, were his subjects for those iconic children.

Grandmom's bathroom was painted seashell pink, with a great big clawfoot bathtub that had white porcelain hot-and-cold knobs. It also had an extra door that door led to the rooftop of the apartment below her.

Grandmom had wonderful large hands for the little, but big, lady she was. They were wrinkled with age, blue veins popping out on the backs of them. She still wore her wedding rings (a size ten, I believe) even though her last husband died in 1952. She loved the large, thin gold wedding band and matching engagement ring with its tiny diamond. She also wore an aquamarine pinky ring on her right hand. That was her birthstone. December 11, 1891, was her birthday.

Grandmom was a neat old lady, always gentle and kind. Though she was strict in her own way, I never thought of crossing her. She was never rich. She never had a television. She never drove a car. I can remember meeting her at the corner when she got off the city bus. She would smile, wave, and then waddle across the street. Her heavy black coat with the broach on the shoulder, and of course a hat, always a hat, kept the chilly wind at bay. I would hug her rotund girth and kind of bounce off her. She was always glad to see me. She was quiet and happy.

Grandmom loved to make pies at Thanksgiving and Christmas. She would come to our house and make them for my mother. I can still see the pies lined up on the radiator cover beneath the kitchen window—pumpkin, mince, apple, cherry—with their browned edges, bubbling fruit, and wonderful aroma. Pumpkin was her favorite. I remember her letting me make the slits in the top of the pies, "A" for apple, "C" for cherry, and other designs on the pie tops. I still use her pumpkin pie recipe today and crimp the edges of my pies the way her large, deft hands taught me years ago.

One afternoon, when I was about ten years old, Grandmom was babysitting me. We were in our sunlit living room. She sat in a red velvet wing chair, twisting her handkerchief in her hands. She looked up and said to me, "When I was eleven years old, I had scarlet fever. All my hair fell out!" She raised her hands and touched her hair. "And look how God blessed me with this full head of hair!" I agreed, as she slid one of the rhinestone combs to the back of her head.

"I remember when I was very sick," Grandmom continued, "I walked down a long, dark hallway. Then, I came to a lion." Her eyes raised, looking into the distance, seemingly way beyond the room. "Then the lion said to me, 'Go back! I don't need you yet.'" Grandmom turned and looked at me. "And after that I got better."

Jesus is known as the Lion of Judah. I still get chills when I recall her story. I know that God's hand was on her life.

I never heard Grandmom complain. I can see her at our kitchen table one hot summer day, sweating like a turkey and mopping her brow with a dainty linen handkerchief, saying, "My, it's warm." The lady was plain old hot, but she never complained. Years later, Dad bought a room air conditioner for our kitchen.

Grandmom loved her church. She had great faith in God. I can still hear her mellow alto voice singing hymns in our living room while I played the piano. She loved music, flowers, and the color red. She also loved people, especially babies.

After I married, I saw less and less of Grandmom. I noticed her starting to fail, walking slower and slower. It was now my job to bring the holiday pies. Vividly, I can see her trying to help clear the table after dinner. Instead of walking around the table to collect the dinnerware, she would pull the tablecloth toward her. Plates would rattle, glasses clink, and silverware fall. I do believe she was trying her best.

Grandmom lived by herself in her apartment above the bakery, on a noisy city street, until she died there, of old age, at the age of eighty-eight. She left this life she loved on December 21, 1979; weirdly, this was exactly forty years after her second husband's death. I have always regretted not attending her funeral. I had just had my third child, Gavin, the week before and could not make the trip to Philadelphia. Funny, my first vivid memory of Grandmom was on a Christmas Eve, and she was buried on Christmas Eve. I never got to say good-bye to her.

Recorded in my memory for my role as a grandmother are Grandmom's gentle ways, her zest for life, her love of tradition, and her great faith and knowledge that God was always with her. I never did anything spectacular with Grandmom; I never went on a trip with her or to the park or the zoo, but she was always there. She would listen to me. She was always Grandmom, with the comforting consistency of being the same all the time. She was my first grown-up friend. If I can follow in her footsteps and give to others what she gave to me, I will consider it an honor.

Guidance

A mother am I
not once
but a handful of times.
Each new babe,
Squirming in my arms
Loved by me,
their Daddy, and Our
Father.
Seasons flee,
calendars change,
children glide through
the echelons of life.
Wisdom needed
desperately
to guide these gifts
is received through
bended knee.
At last, me, their Daddy,
and Our Father
have led
these lambs through
their growing years,
'til they became
parents themselves.

The Orchid Widow

1974

When I open my eyes, the sky outside the window is dark gray. Green gingham curtains float back and forth as the wind blows the thin glass of the window. I fling back the covers, roll onto my side and off the bed, and stand up. I am so excited today!

It is a rainy January day, but I dress quickly. I put on one of the four tops that fit me, a cranberry red one I got for Christmas. I use the bedpost to help keep my balance as I step into navy blue slacks and pull them up over my big tummy.

Bill, my husband, is in the kitchen of our tiny apartment, making coffee. I give him a hug and a kiss.

"Good morning!" I say. "Anne's coming down today. I'm meeting her at your mom's house. I am so happy I will have a friend to talk to!" I look out at the rain hitting the window. "Maybe we will go over to the mall." I smile at Bill, look away, and then add, "I don't have any money, but it's always fun to look."

"The mall is probably a good idea, with the weather like it is." He goes into the hallway and gets a box of cereal out of the closet where we keep everything from cereal to toilet paper. He pours corn flakes into a bowl and adds some milk. I join him at our table and hold his hand as he says grace.

Then he reaches in his back pocket and pulls out his wallet. "I'll give you what I have," he says, but there is no money in his wallet. "Oh, that's right, I spent the last money I had on the milk and eggs I picked up on the way home the other day."

"That's okay, I don't need any money."

"I'm sorry," he said.

Bill gets up and pours my coffee. It smells so good. A few months ago, I couldn't stand the smell of it; pregnancy does funny things to a girl.

I slide my hand over the top of the small kitchen table, past the red and yellow placemat. I like this ice cream table; Bill made it. He found the base in the barn at his family's greenhouse business. He cut a new piece of wood for the top, refinished the metal wrought iron legs, and painted it white. My mom gave us two old chairs that Bill painted white to complete our kitchen set. It is just right.

"We have to set up the baby's things soon," I said. I pop some bread into the toaster.

Bill adds milk and sugar to his coffee and stirs with his entire arm, around and around. The vortex of the coffee reaches the top of the mug, then subsides. His coffee is the color of liquid peanut butter.

"We have time, don't we?" Bill asks.

"Probably. I figure the baby is due around February 3."

"Plenty of time!" he says. He butters the two pieces of toast.

We recently put the crib up in the small second bedroom. It is full of the gift boxes of tiny outfits, blankets, lotions, and powders I received as shower gifts. I must wash those little clothes and set up the changing able my cousin gave me.

The changing table has five wicker "drawers" and a thick vinyl pad on top. It folds together when not in use, the drawers meshing between each other, one on top of the other. The dressing table, boxes of cloth diapers, and an infant seat are now behind the headboard of our double bed, which fits caddie-corner in our small bedroom, leaving a perfect space for storage.

After breakfast, I put on my two-tone brown suede saddle shoes with red soles. I love these shoes, but they are hard to reach to tie in my condition. My blue jacket doesn't quite close in the front.

Bill and I drive through Ocean City from our apartment at 56th Street and turn west on 9th Street. It is winter and desolate here. We stop at a traffic light, even though there are no cars at the cross street, no cars anywhere.

"I talked to Mrs. Churchville, and she said she would be with me when the baby comes. I hope she can get here in time," I say to Bill. We turn onto the Ocean City 9th Street bridge.

Mrs. Churchville is a lovely African American lady at our church who helps deliver babies. She lives in Philadelphia.

"My mom would help you too, ya know," Bill says as he takes his eye off the barren road and looks at me. "She's delivered babies."

"I know." I look out the side window, yanking my coat tighter over my belly. I think that's a little weird, having your mother-in-law deliver your baby, but I can't say that to Bill. He's tied real close to his family. Besides, he's a guy, and guys just don't get it. God will have to help me get through this one.

Bill doesn't say anything as he eyes the road. A bell clangs. We slow down and stop as red lights flash and a red and white barrier arm drops in front of us. The bridge is opening. No other cars are on the bridge this cold, rainy Friday morning, but a blue and white cabin cruiser with a huge flying bridge sounds its horn as he heads under the raised drawbridge, out of the bay toward the ocean. Going fishing, I guess.

We pull into Mom's driveway and see Anne's car there already. Bill and I climb the flagstone steps of the porch to the kitchen door of the huge stone house where Bill himself was born.

Bill's mother, Elizabeth, along with Anne and Mrs. Williams, Mom's housekeeper, greet us. Mrs. Williams' nickname is "Wums." (When Bill's brother, George, was little, he could not pronounce the name Williams, and he said "Wums" instead. The name stuck.)

"Hi!" I say. I give them each a hug. Bill does too.

"You must have gotten up early to be here by now," I say to Anne.

"Well, I am an early bird, you know. As soon as Frankie went to work, I was off and running," Anne says.

Anne is married to my brother, Frankie, and they live in Roslyn, Pennsylvania, about seventy miles away. Bill and Anne are also cousins. Frankie introduced Bill and me to each other.

Mom puts her raincoat on and says, "I must get to work now, but all of you come back for dinner around five. It's just something quick. Remember, we are having a bridal shower here for Beverly tonight." Mom heads out the door and goes down the flagstone path that leads to the greenhouses.

"Where do you want to go today?" Anne asks.

"I thought we could roam around the mall."

"That would be great. Then, maybe we could also have lunch somewhere," Anne says.

"Er, yeah, that's good," I say. I look at the floor. Oh, gosh, how am I going to pay for lunch?

"Wums, would you like to come shopping with us?" Anne asks.

"Me? Well . . . yes, I would!" Wums says and nods her head. "I'll go and get my coat."

"Bill, why don't you come to lunch with us?" Anne asks. "That would be fun! Come on, you can't work all the time. Besides, it's *my* treat!" She smiles and winks at me, then continues. "Surely, Bill, you can leave that business for an hour to have lunch with us."

I smile at Anne, because she said exactly what I was thinking. Everyone knows Bill works too much at this greenhouse business. Six days a week, and one Sunday a month. I look at Bill's blue eyes; they crinkle at the edges as he takes the ribbing from his cousin. He looks at the floor, debating if his folks would approve of his leaving work in the middle of the day. He looks up and sees me smiling. I am holding my breath waiting for his answer. Blue eyes meet blue eyes. I wonder if he feels my excitement that we would be going to a restaurant!

He smiles, "Yeah, cuz, that would be great! See you around 1:00 at the diner on the circle."

*   *   *

Anne, Wums, and I come out of the mall. We walked from one end of the mall to the other, but only Wums bought something.

"Let me go get the car, so we all won't get wet," Anne says. She pulls up the hood of her raincoat and waits for a few cars to pass. Then, she sprints around deep puddles to her car.

"Beverly will love those towels you bought," I say to Wums.

"I hope so. I know she likes yellow. She can always use another set of towels, too." Wums smiles and pats the carry-all bag. "They even wrapped them for me."

"They did a beautiful job, too. It is a perfect gift."

Anne pulls the car to the curb. I open the front door for Wums, then climb into the back seat myself.

"We'll be at the diner just in time," Anne says. She steps on the gas and exits the mall parking lot.

Up front, Anne and Wums talk, while I settle back, stretch out my legs, and watch the tiny raindrops hit the window, then squiggle down and sideways along the glass. The heat in the car is kicking in, and I feel its warmth surround me.

I think of the great time we had at the mall. ***Thank you, Lord, for these wonderful friends and Your blessing.*** *The baby kicks.* ***Also, thank you, Lord, for this little one. I smile and cannot help but think that this little baby knows what I am thinking. Bless us with Your presence throughout today.***

We stop at a traffic light. I see a woman carry a child quickly across the street, shielding her from the rain. Then I remember the baby bottles I saw today: three of them. Three random bottles!

The first bottle was on the ledge of the outside display window when we walked into Sears. There was no one around. The bottle was just left there. I thought, "Uh-oh, that poor baby."

Then, I looked at coats in the ladies department. On top of one of the circular racks was another baby bottle! No one was near, no child anywhere. I get a tingling along my neck when I think about it now.

About an hour later, Anne went to the hardware department, and I went to look at the housewares. There, on a shelf, next to some baking dishes, was another baby bottle! I clasp my hands together now and close my eyes and think what those bottles could mean. Could God be sending me a message? I do wonder…

*God uses the number three a lot. It is one of His favorite numbers. The trinity is **three**, the Father, Son, and Holy Spirit. The **three** Hebrew children, Shadrach, Meshach, and Abednego, who were thrown into a fiery furnace because they would not bow down and worship a golden idol—but God protected them, and they did not burn or even smell like smoke. Then, Jesus rose from the grave after **three** days.*

Hmmm …

*The baby kicks hard three times. I smile and place my hand on my belly. Maybe it means our family, the three of us—Bill, me, and our baby. Maybe, God wants me to know that He is answering my prayers. He **is** blessing us with His presence all day. **Thank you, Lord, for Your goodness to me.***

I don't tell Anne or Wums about the bottles. I ponder them deep in my heart. Seeing them seems precious to me now. I recall reading, when Jesus was born, Mary also pondered things in her heart—the shepherds, the wise men, the gifts. A mother's heart—I guess that is what I too have, even now.

Bill meets us at the Point Diner. We sit in a booth that overlooks the Great Egg Harbor Bay. The bay is gray and choppy, the wind blowing the top of the waves, peeling back their white water. The cold rain blows against the window, but the diner is warm. It smells like cinnamon buns. A lady in the next booth walks to the juke box and deposits some coins. A minute later, Neil Diamond sings *Solitary Man*. We order lunch. It seems like a long time since I ate breakfast.

I lean back against the green vinyl seat and wrap my hand around my warm mug of coffee. Anne tells Bill about the orchid nursery where she works in Pennsylvania. Wums and I talk about the shower for Beverly. She said she made an apricot cheesecake, Beverly's favorite.

Our food comes and I devour the grilled cheese sandwich and cup of vegetable soup. Bill and I tell Anne and Wums all about the free childbirth classes we have been taking in Cape May Court House. These classes are so interesting.

"I asked Mrs. Churchville to be with me. She said she would come when I need her," I say.

"Mrs. Churchville probably learned how to deliver babies from her aunt, Mrs. Williams here. Wums has delivered babies," Anne says as she smiles and nudges Wums.

"Yeah, but that was in my younger years. I don't do it anymore." Wums laughs. "Anne Churchville is good, she'll be fine with you ... if she doesn't get lost getting to your place."

"Oh yeah, Debby, Mrs. Churchville always gets lost," Bill says. He flattens the napkin against the table several times.

Anne nods. "She does do that ... a lot."

"Oh boy, I hope not when we need her," I say. I look at Bill. He shrugs.

"We'll see what happens," he says.

"I think you guys could have this baby by yourselves, after hearing you talk about those classes," Anne says.

"Not really," I laugh. "I have read a lot about it, though. God will have to take care of us and this baby, that's all."

We finish our meal and get up from the table.

"He will," Wums whispers to me as I get my coat on. She pats my back. "Yes, He will! Yessir, He will."

*   *   *

The large living room is crowded. Wrapping paper and bows cover the floor, and laughter and cackling fills the room. It is a happy night. I talk to my good friends, Claudia and Denise, and Mrs. Churchville. She laughs and says I'm getting big.

I sit on the hassock near the gigantic stone fireplace; the heat from it feels good. I watch Beverly open her gifts. I sit up straight and rub my back and think how much I love these people. We are from all over New Jersey and the Philadelphia area, but we have a strong bond. We go to the same church in Philadelphia. Christian fellowship is what it is—there is no bond like it. I wish more of them lived near me. I really need to find a good friend around here.

Last year, I moved to Ocean City, and I have not found a good friend yet. I need someone to talk to like I talk to these girls. I need a friend to do things with. I love our apartment and being married to Bill. However, phone calls home to my mom or any of these girls just cost too much money. I do talk to my mom and dad every couple of days. However, I don't tell my mom a lot of things; like how I don't always feel like I belong here with Bill's family—*that* especially bothers me. They are so involved with working at the business, they don't even seem to care about me. My mother would not like that. I don't know what I did wrong, except marry their son. My Mom has told me to "make a life for yourself," because Bill's life is his work. Sigh. It is hard to do, Mom. I guess I must try harder.

Hmmmm … I surface from my thoughts and look across the room.

The hot fire crackles, and on the other side of the coffee table Beverly holds up a large, beautiful vase. I smile and realize how happy I am here with my friends.

Ida, Bill's sister, waves to me from across the room, indicating that dessert is ready whenever Beverly finishes opening her gifts. I straighten my back and stretch a bit and nod to her. Then Ida disappears into the kitchen.

I sink back into my thoughts.

Bill's family are great people, but I am the outsider, the odd piece to the puzzle. His parents, brothers, and sister are all busy and involved with the orchid business. I am not. I have nothing in common with them—except my Bill.

When I stopped in at the greenhouses to drop lunch off for Bill, everyone was working, cutting and packing orchids in boxes for shipping. I said "hi," and talked to them. They answered, but never stopped their work, or even turned to look at me. It is just strange that *my Bill*, his folks, and siblings all do the *same* thing. It is almost like they're afraid to stop work; their work is *their everything*.

It's just weird.

I have mentioned this to Bill, and he says they all have things to do; but I don't think it's nice. Sometimes I *do* wonder if they like me or not, but I try not to think about it.

Beverly finishes opening her gifts, and everyone heads to the dining room. I am too tired to go, so I move from the hassock to the sofa and put my feet up. I will get something to eat in a bit. I lay my head back, and for some reason, my thoughts go to yesterday morning.

Most days, I keep myself busy. I walk four blocks to the beach, then usually walk to the south point of the island. A lot of the houses here at the south end of the island are summer houses. There are only three year-round people on my street; no one is my age. I get lonely. In winter it is strange that there is no one living in most of these houses. Nights are especially eerie. The streets are very dark.

The sun is warm for January, but it's windy. I bundle up the best I can and walk to the beach. I like to walk here; it is my time to think and pray. I always feel better when I get home.

Today, I feel like the Michelin man; my skin is stretched tight in all directions, my clothes outline the round bulges of my body just like that tire hero. My arms fill out my jacket sleeves; the button of my jacket is bursting from boobs I never knew could get so big. With a stomach that is surely at its breaking point, I beat the Michelin man's girth. I rub my belly and think, this baby must come sometime soon.

I step up the curb of the beach block. Not only does my jacket not close but, as I look down, the jacket opening forms a great "V" shape, buttoned at my chest, then splaying outward, open a foot in each direction. I look like a huge circus tent, its door flapping open in the wind. All I need are some stripes, a flag on my head, and a sign: Fat Lady Exhibit. The worst part is that I waddle from side to side.

I laugh at myself now, because whenever I see the Michelin man, he is happy. If a guy who looks like a white, trussed marshmallow can smile . . . so can I. I know God wants me to be happy. He loves me, that's what the Bible promises. I will pray for more happiness, and I will pray for a girlfriend too. That is what I'll do.

The herring gulls scream overhead, and a stiff gust of wind yanks blonde strands of hair out of my ponytail. I tuck them behind my ear, only to have them whip across my face again. On my left, between two houses, is a sailboat cocooned in gray canvas, hibernating for the winter. Its halyards flap continuously against its partially wrapped mast. The tolling sound echoes down the empty beach. Over the tarred, wooden bulkhead I see plumes of white sea spray blow high into the air from the rows of breakers, then the waves wash back to the sea.

I climb the short flight of steps up and then down over the bulkhead. I head south on the desolate beach toward the point of Corson's Inlet. The wind at my back feels like a big hand pushing me down the beach. They say a lost child on the beach will always walk with the wind. Sometimes I feel like that child—lost—like I do not belong here. I complain too much, I know I do... Bill wants me to be happy while he is at work, but it's hard. I haven't made any friends. I miss my family. I guess I'm jealous; he sees his every day.

I had a job last summer at a local school. I worked with some older women, no one my age. I miss working, and I miss the money. One day last fall, I stopped at the greenhouse. Everyone was so busy. I asked Bill if I could help pack the orchids for delivery. He looked at me, then turned away. I saw him look to his folks for approval. He frowned, and his voice said, "I don't think you could do the job right." But his sad blue eyes told me a different story.

I turned away, got in the car, and went home.

When Bill got home that night, he hugged me for a long time; neither one of us said anything. We never talked about it again.

I do not like to think of that time. I do love him, but he hurt my feelings a lot. I just cannot interfere with Bill and that business.

Orchids, schmorchids.

In this foreign land, Bill is my anchor. A man is supposed to leave his father and mother and cleave to his wife. That's what the good book says. God will have to help me with this one, too.

Breaking waves pound at the point where the ocean and Corson's Inlet merge. I have been walking for over an hour already. I scan the inlet. There is nothing except the sea, the sky, and the sand. I turn and head toward home.

I love these walks, this think time. I talk to God. Sometimes He answers me right away. Sometimes I must wait. But He always listens. I am glad He listens. Now, I feel ashamed of my feelings. Here I am, twenty years old, acting like a brat. I should not get so mad at things that happen. I should not get upset at people I'm supposed to love. I should not complain. I have a wonderful life. I just have to find my own friends, friends who care.

I kick at three clam shells, right in a row. The last one is filled with a smelly, slimy clam and oozy putrid water soaks my shoes and pants.

"Ugh, oh crap. What a mess!" The smell of rotten clam juice curdles my nose.

I hold my belly as I bend to wipe the muck off my shoes and pants with a piece of conch shell. I waddle away fast to get away from the smell, but I get out of breath and must stop. I inhale deeply—clean, cold, salt air—filling my lungs again and again.

"I won't let it bother me anymore," I promise myself. "I have a wonderful life, a wonderful home, and a terrific, loving husband. Lord, forgive me!"

My jacket flaps in the wind. I am getting cold. I see the zig-zagging trail of my earlier footprints on the sand. Seagulls squawk overhead, probably thinking my leg is a big piece of garbage because of its smell. I shoo them away, flapping my arms like one of them. They fly off. As the waves recede, a bunch of sandpipers scurry toward the ocean, pecking at the sand, racing back up the beach when another wave breaks. They are fast.

I look out toward the ocean and watch a lone fisherman at the end of the 59th Street fishing pier. I shield my eyes against the bright sun and see his silhouette. He is reeling in a fish. It is a foot or more long, probably a tautog. They are good, tasting like chicken when they're cooked up.

On this lonely beach, I pray for forgiveness, for more happiness, for a friend, and, of course, for Bill and our little baby. I know God hears me. I hope He understands this lonely girl whose emotions go from happy to sad very quickly. God will answer my prayers.

As I waddle on, I feel a great peace come over me. I smile at a bunch of squawking seagulls standing on the sand, crusted from high tide, in three perfect rows facing the wind. Their pure white feathers splay flat against their chests, like sailors at attention in dress-whites. I laugh at them; they are so cute.

On the walk back home, the beach seems longer and the wind stronger. My eyes are tiny slits now, filtering the sun and blowing sand. A ship is on the horizon, turning, heading out to sea. I *finally climb over the bulkhead to the street. With every step of my right foot, I get a whiff of rotten clams.*

I climb the long flight of steps to our apartment, leaving my shoes and socks outside on the porch. Inside our warm little home, I change my clothes. Later, I open the sliding door and put my "clammy" pants outside too. PeeeeUuuuu! I will wash them later.

I close the door quickly and turn to the small sun-filled kitchen. Suddenly, the heat in the room envelops me in radiant warmth. With wonder, I fill the tea kettle and set a mug on the table. I smile and know that God is with me. I make a cheese sandwich for lunch and, of course, vegetable soup, the kind with the little alphabet letters. I have eaten alphabet soup almost every lunch since I have been pregnant. Maybe, our baby will be a great reader, nourished with all those little letters.

"Debby!" Beverly calls from the dining room, "Come! Have some of this cheesecake!"

"I'm coming right now!" I say as I wake up my tired body. Sitting on the edge of the sofa, I rock back and forth a few times and on the third try, I stand up. I am tired, but I had such a great day being with Anne and all my friends. I head to the dining room for some of that cheesecake and a cup of tea with the girls.

*   *   *

On our way home to Ocean City, Bill says he plans to take tomorrow, Saturday, off from work. Our church group is meeting in northern New Jersey to go ice skating, but he can't decide whether to go. The guys like to play ice hockey.

We girls just skate around. Well, not me, not now. I would like to go, but I'm really tired.

I know Bill wants to go, but he doesn't want to leave me. I tell him to go and have fun! We pull into the dark alley that leads to our driveway. At the third driveway on the left, Bill parks on the cement slab. I open the door and try to maneuver gracefully out of the car. Bill gets out of the car and slams the door.

"OOwww! Ohh, Sheeeeezz!!" Bill screams and screams. I hear the door open and shut again. I see him running around the front of the car, slinging his arms furiously up and down. He races up the outside wooden steps two at a time.

I run after Bill up the steps and across the wide porch. When I open the sliding glass door, Bill is hanging his arm over the kitchen sink, blood gushing furiously out of his finger. He seems weak and leans on the counter.

"What happened!!?" I yell.

"I slammed the car door on my finger! Ohhhh," He sucks in his breath and closes his eyes; his face is white.

"Run it under cold water," I say as I rush past him.

I run to the hall closet and grab a clean washcloth, put some ice in it, and wrap it around the ring finger of his left hand. The white quick of the nail bed is protruding beyond the end of his nail. I have to look away as I wrap it up.

"I'll be okay," Bill says. "It feels better wrapped up like that."

"Gosh, you scared me, Bill," I say as I rub his back. He turns from the sink and goes into the bedroom. I look at the clock. It is twelve midnight. Suddenly, I am very, very tired.

Bill lies on the bed, his bandaged hand straight up in the air. I give him a fresh cloth with ice in it and put the bloody cloth in the sink in the bathroom.

Ten minutes later, I come out of the bathroom.

"Bill," I say. "Bill!"

"What is it?"

"I think the baby's coming!"

Bill springs up from the bed. His eyes are bright and the color seems to have miraculously flowed back into his face. His cheeks are ruddy again, his eyes wide. Maybe his finger does not hurt any more.

"What d'ya mean? How'd you know?" Bill runs to me. "What should I do?"

"I had a showing."

"Oh, what's a showing again? Does that come first? Showing, contractions, transition, push, breathe. I am getting them all twisted up. Oh, crap, I cannot remember what a showing is!"

"Bill, calm down."

"What do we do now?"

"Call your Mom's house and see if Mrs. Churchville is still there. I hope she is. There would be no way to get hold of her if she's on her way back to Philly."

Bill dashes to the kitchen, knocking his finger against the door jamb.

"Ooowwww, boy does that hurt!"

He dials Mom on the yellow wall phone hanging in the kitchen. In a blur, I start wondering what, exactly, I should do next. I stand and brace my tummy and breathe long slow breaths. Then I go to the hall closet and grab a large flannel-backed rubber sheet. I hear Bill talking to his mom, but I cannot hear what he's saying. Darn, all those Off's talk so softly.

I go to the bedroom. Just yesterday I had put a new set of clean sheets on our bed. The large rubber sheet goes over those clean sheets, flannel side up. I lay a couple of towels on top of that, and a clean flat sheet on top. I try to tuck in the sheet as best I can . . . oh, forget it. I gotta stop. I sit on the bed and breathe deeply through another contraction. Where is Bill? I tune my ear to towards the kitchen and hear him talking about his finger! *Oh, Lord, his mom does not have to know about that now!*

"Bill!! What are you doing?" I yell. "Did you forget me? Come here!"

I go to the bathroom; I think I have to pee, but I don't. Bill comes in as I am standing by the sink and hears me groan as I hold my stomach.

"Ah, Debby, let me rub your back," he says and leans toward me.

"No! Get away from me! I don't need your help!" I take a swing at his arm.

Bill starts shouting, "You are halfway there! The baby *is* coming. I do remember what transition is, and you are in it. You do not want anything to do with me and you are acting like an angry witch. That is transition!" He smiles radiantly as he looks at me.

Is this guy for real? I look at him and slam the bathroom door shut. I am so mad at him. He is loony. Breathe out slowly, breathe in, o--u--t and i--n. When the contraction is over, I put on my pale pink nightgown. For some reason, I want to look pretty. I guess I am loony too.

"Is Mrs. Churchville coming?" I ask as I hobble out of the bathroom.

"No, she left. But my mom is headed over."

Oh brother. This is going to be awkward. **Lord, help me.**

I quickly forget about Mom and think I had better get in bed; I don't feel good. I feel heavy.

I lie in bed on my side. Bill comes and faces me and breathes with me when the contractions come. Twenty minutes later, I hear Mom's car pull up in the driveway.

The sliding door opens. I hear Mom take off her jacket. She comes into the bedroom.

"Sorry, to put you through all this," I say. I look away. I am so embarrassed.

"Don't you worry about that, how are you feeling?" She looks at me as Bill and I breathe through a long contraction.

"Bill, can you put a pot of water on to boil? I must sterilize the scissors."

Bill heads to the kitchen.

"Would you mind if I look to see how far along you are?" she asks. Suddenly, I find that soft voice very comforting.

Mom sees my embarrassment I guess, but I spread my legs for her to see.

"Aw, don't worry, we all look alike. We girls gotta stick together," she says. Her words send more comfort to me. I relax and concentrate on having this baby.

Bill comes back. I breathe hard again.

"Mom, I feel like I have to push."

"Uuum, can you wait a bit? It is not quite time," she says quietly.

I have another hard contraction.

"Mom, I have to push. This baby is coming!" I grab the outside of my thighs. Bill is behind me bracing my shoulders. I push hard until I think my guts are going to rip open.

"Debby, you can do this. You are doing great," Bill says.

I drop my head back against his chest and, suddenly, I want my mother. Tears cloud my vision.

"Bill, here we go again," I say. I bear down with all that is left in me.

"Ohhhh," I catch my breath for only a half a second before another contraction comes.

I push hard again and then again. Then, my water breaks, and the baby's head slides out quickly, then the shoulders. Squirming hips and legs come next with furious loud crying. The baby slides right into Mom's arms. I never knew a sound could bring such joy. I am crying and Bill is too. Crying and laughing at this pink naked screaming baby.

" It's a girl," Mom says. She wraps her in a soft baby towel and lays her on my chest, adding, "Wow, she was quick! It is two o'clock."

A short time later, I deliver the afterbirth. Mom tells Bill how to cut the umbilical cord. By law, she tells us, one parent of the child is supposed to cut the cord. Once the cord stops pumping food and oxygen to the baby, Bill ties a string around the cord close to the baby's tummy. Then he ties another string two inches from the first. Bill takes the boiled, cooled scissors and cuts between the strings.

Mom cleans the baby up and weighs and measures her: 7 pounds, 3 ounces, 19 inches long!

Bill climbs over my head and reaches a box of diapers behind the bed. He brings some boxes from the crib with baby outfits. I choose a yellow nightgown "sacque" for her with tiny pale peach bunnies on it. The baby had stopped crying, but now starts again. Mom dresses her quickly, wraps her in a white blanket and holds her against her shoulder.

I roll over to one side of the bed and Bill gathers the towels and puts them in a large bag for the laundry. The rubber sheet goes in the trash.

Mom gives the baby to Bill to hold. She helps me get cleaned up. I put on a clean nightgown, a blue one this time. I wiggle under the top sheet. Bill props up some pillows behind my back.

Now, I hold our little girl, who is wrapped tight, sucking her thumb. I finally have a chance to get a good look at her. She is pink with a head of soft, downy, light brown hair. I kiss her head and hold her tiny hand. She looks all around with big blue-gray eyes. She has the roundest, most beautiful face I have ever seen. She is beautiful, just beautiful! My heart is bursting with love for her already. *Thank you, God, for this beautiful baby girl!*

Wums was right; God did take care of us. He always does.

"Why don't you two try to get some sleep? I will sterilize a bottle and some water for her for later."

"I'm just going to hold her for a while," I say. Then I add, "Mom . . . thank you for everything, for your help and for being here." I smile at her, and suddenly I just love that humble woman standing at the foot of our bed. "I love you, Mom," I say. My eyes get blurry. I look down at the baby.

"I love you too," Mom says. "I'm glad I was here. That little girl came really fast! She's my first grandchild, and she's beautiful!" She smiles at the baby. "I'll be back in a few minutes. I will take care of the baby through the night so you both can get some sleep."

"Yeah, Mom," Bill says, "thanks so much for your help. I wouldn't have known what to do."

She laughs, smiles, and says, "God took care of all of us tonight." Then, she walks quietly down the hall.

Bill turns the lamp light low and climbs into bed next to me. He kisses our baby and gives me a long kiss. "I love you, Billy. Thank you so much for your strength and your love for me and now this little girl! I'm sorry I've been so cranky."

"You're not cranky ... er, not now, anyway," He laughs. "We have a beautiful baby girl. Thank you. You are the best," he says as he pulls the covers up.

I cannot even think of sleeping. The baby sucks her thumb and sleeps in my arms. What a wonderful feeling, holding a sleeping baby.

A while later, Mom comes into the room quietly and takes the baby to the living room.

I keep thinking back on the day: my visit with Anne and my friends, those mysterious baby bottles, the shower, and this gorgeous little baby girl with no name. *Thank you, Lord, for being so good to us.* I pray for a long time.

"Ugggh," Bill rolls over on his back, then his side; then he shakes his bandaged hand. The bed bounces with his restlessness. He groans again and again, tossing and turning.

"Bill, are you okay?" I finally say.

"My finger throbs and throbs," he says.

"Ahh, I'm sorry," I turn and hug him. "How can I help?"

"I will be all right, once I get to sleep," he says. "But ohhhh, does it hurt!"

"I know it does," I say. I turn away and roll my eyes in the dim light of the room. I'm the one who just had a baby ... and his finger hurts! Then I smile, turn back, and look at him curled under the blankets, his wavy dark hair on the pillow, and suddenly I just love this guy more than ever. I reach over and hold his "good" hand.

I still cannot sleep. I just cannot wait until my mother and father come. When Bill called my parents just after two o'clock, my mother answered the phone.

"We have a little girl!" Bill said.

"Oh, oh, oh! You must be busy! Good-bye!" And she hung up!

I laugh out loud as I recall this. They will be here in the morning from Pennsylvania.

Bill groans and turns over again.

Lord, thank you for giving us our little girl, this beautiful little daughter. I prayed for a new friend, and You have sent her to me.

We will name her Wendy Brooke. Yes, "Wendy Brooke Off." It is the perfect name for our little bundle of joy.

Fluffer-frumpers

I follow the sound of giggles and squeals. I go up the short flight of stairs to the upstairs and stand in the doorway of the hall bathroom. I laugh at Bill because he is always such a hoot to watch.

Bill has the two girls, Abbey and Cami, sitting on the counter, one on each side of the sink, brushing their teeth. Bill is armed with a small purple toothbrush that is white and foamy, matching Cami's lips and chin.

My heart could just burst open with my love for him. He has so much to deal with at the business, especially this week. And here he is brushing little teeth like he's doing the most important job in the world.

*   *   *

Oh Lord, bless my Bill today, and give him help in dealing with his work and family.

George, Bill's brother, is ten years younger than Bill. He went wayward as a teenager and has made some bad choices over the last ten years to support his drug habit. He has stolen valuables from his parents, family, and our business to support that habit; but the family never pressed charges against him. Six months ago, he went to jail for robbing someone else. George got out of jail yesterday, and he's back home living with Bill's folks. They are glad he's out of prison, as I guess any parent would be. I know they have been praying that he would change his bad ways—we all have been praying that prayer.

However, when George is around, everyone is on edge. He can't be trusted. If anyone questions him, he flies off the handle. Then, family or business things "show up" missing. He's slick enough to cover his tracks most of the time; and if George is caught by family, there are no consequences for him.

Bill is frowned upon because he doesn't want George back working at the business. The family says Bill should forgive his brother and have compassion on him.

Bill works so hard, but for what? Anything gained is stolen. This has gone on for many, many years. Bill's family had George working at the greenhouse the last time he got out of the "slammer" a few years back, then he stole from us again.

Last year George sold his yellow Camaro to one of his friends. Two days later, his friend stopped by the greenhouse and asked to talk to Bill. This friend said he had something Bill might want. He opened the trunk of the Camaro. Inside were two large boxes of sterling-silver-engraved trophies and sterling loving cups that Bill's dad had won for his displays in the Philadelphia Flower Show in the 1940s and '50s. I guess George forgot he stole them and didn't take them to the pawn shop. At least, George's friend was honest. Bill brought the boxes of trophies home to our house, so George wouldn't be any wiser.

So, George is back home. I could just cry . . .we'll see what's next.

Lord, I know and pray that You can change George, if he wants to change. But please help Bill deal with all this today. Bill is such a good, good man. Lord, I need Your help too.

*   *   *

The purple toothbrush is aimed at Cami's foamy back molars. Bill closes one eye to inspect them.

"Ah-ha!! There goes a fluffer-frumper!!" Bill swishes the brush on the molars with a quick stroke.

"I got that one! But wait, there's another on the bottom!" The purple brush moves lightning fast through the white foam. "We got that one too!"

"Dad-dee, luffe-umper!!" Cami says. "Do 'gain!" She kicks her feet against the cabinet, claps her hands, then wipes her face with an open hand, and opens her mouth wide again.

"No, it'th my turn!" Abbey says. "My turn!" She tries to grab the toothbrush, but Bill holds it high in the air. "Dad-dee!" she shrieks as she reaches high.

"Hang on a minute, Abs, I think I see one more fluffer-frumper running around Cami's teeth. I'll get that bad guy!" He whisks the purple brush gently across Cami's few front teeth.

"I got him! That fluffer-frumper is gone!" He tips her head back, closes one eye, and looks at the top of her mouth like a pirate looking through a spy glass. "Hmmmm, very interesting ... hmmm." Bill pulls her chin down, then he drops his chin to his chest and looks out the top of his eyes at the bottom teeth.

"Ummmm, yes, aahhh," he says, still searching for fluffer-frumpers. Her eyes are as wide open as her mouth.

"Ahhh, yes, yes, hmmmmmm … " Without turning his head, Bill turns on the cold water tap and rinses the purple brush.

"Voila! I declare the fluffer-frumpers are gone!" He puts one hand on the top of her head and one hand on her chin and clomps her mouth shut. With a whisk of his little purple magic wand toothbrush, he sprinkles cold water on her.

"Dad-d-deee!" Cami yells, rubbing her hands through her long blonde hair.

"Now, you may have a sip of water!" Bill gives Cami a tiny teacup filled with water from their tea set on the counter.

"Daddy, come on! You're takin' too long!" Abbey grabs the purple brush from his hand and throws it in the sink. This sends Cami, then Abbey too, into howls of laughter.

"Shhh, this is very important," Bill says, as he pulls up his sleeves. He dots the bristles of Abbey's pink toothbrush with toothpaste, then lifts the tube quickly and forms a perfect ice cream cone curlicue on the brush.

"How'd you do dat?!" Abbey asks. Then laughs, kicking her legs back and forth, her hands hanging onto the edge of the counter.

"Ah, that's my secret; the secret of catching fluffer-frumpers!" Bill brings the bristles up close to his eye and examines the swirly goo, like Sherlock Holmes looking at a clue.

"Now, it is time to get your big FLUFFER-FRUMPERS, Miss Abigail!

ARRRGHH!" He throws both hands over his head in advance of his attack. "Open sezzzz-ammmmeeeee!" Abbey opens her mouth, holding back giggles, and the search begins.

Lord, give ME strength and love to deal with his family too.

"Wow, look at all of them! I got that one," Bill brushes the uppers with quick strokes, "and that one! Hey, there go two on the upper right. Bam! They're done!"

Abbey's eyes are like big blue marbles on top of a crinkled tiny nose. She tries not to laugh. Cami is trying to see in Abbey's mouth too, leaning over the sink.

"Hold on tight, Abs, those bad fluffer-frumpers are almost gone." He zooms the brush in and out of her mouth, across her tiny teeth, with such gentleness in his touch compared to the mission he is on. White bubbles dribble down Abbey's chin as Bill chases the last fluffer-frumper away.

"There!!" With a long wipe of his forehead, Bill says, "We got all of them. What a job! I'm exhausted!" He rinses the magic wand pink toothbrush, then raises it and swirls it through the air, "Presto, you're done!"

Abbey covers her face as water sprinkles around her. "Dadd-deeee!" Abbey shouts.

"Down!" Cami says, raising her arms. Bill's hands circle Cami's waist and he lifts her high in the air with more squeals, then drops her lightly to the ground.

"My turn!" Abbey says.

He does the same airplane lift with her. They both run past me and go down the hallway.

"Did anyone ever tell you, you're a nut?" I ask Bill as I hug him.

Surprised, he turns and says, "Absolutely not! A nut, really?"

Abbey runs by me and goes down the stairs to the living room. Cami follows her, but at the top of the steps, Cami spins around, and flops down each step on her belly until she reaches the living room.

Bill and I head down the steps together.

We go into the kitchen. The smell of coffee is delicious. Even though I've had one cup already, I pour myself another. Bill follows me. He wraps his arms around me.

"Will you be okay today? I worry, ya know?" I hold his large hands and lace my fingers through his.

"My brother got out yesterday," Bill says as he looks through the window at the back yard. The wind blows the swings on the swing set.

"I know."

"They want to hire him again."

"I figured they would. It just doesn't make any sense!" I say as I grip his hands tight and spread my arms wide. "He goes to jail for stealing, and they want to hire him back! I'm sorry but, your family is crazy!"

"Sshh!" Bill says and glances towards the living room. "I know. It is crazy. They say he needs a job. He should go out and get a job somewhere else. Then, they tell me, 'Who would hire him with a record?'"

"Exactly!" I say.

Bill sighs, shrugging his shoulders. "Oh, there's no use talking about it. I'm frustrated enough, and I don't want to upset you."

"It does upset me. Especially that they don't even consider your opinion."

"I know. I'm sorry," Bill smiles, "but, I have you, and the kids. . ." He swings my hands like a guy on his first date.

I laugh. "I love you."

"I'm glad," he says and brushes a kiss on the top of my forehead, smiles and says, "I love you too." He turns and walks to the living room closet and gets his jacket out of the closet.

I get some milk out of the refrigerator and pour it into my coffee and walk to the living room.

"Daddy, don't go!" Abbey yells as she runs across the room and wraps her arms around his leg, then wraps her legs around his leg too.

"I think I'll go to work now, Mom," Bill says. He walks to the door with her clinging to his leg, holding onto him like a koala bear hanging on a tree.

"Dad-dee!"

"I think I'll have to take Abbey with me." He walks around and around the living room with her stuck to his leg.

"No!!" She lets go, runs and flops on the sofa.

Cami toddles to Bill and raises her arms. He lifts her up, "Not doh, daddy, 'tay wiff uth!"

"I have to go to the greenhouse, but we'll play when I get home from work tonight. How about Mommy walks you to the playground now?"

"O-tay," she says as she squiggles out of his arms and runs to the closet and pulls her jacket off the low hook.

"I'll get Abbey's Big Wheel and the stroller out of the garage when I get my bike," he says as he goes out the front door. "I love you," he calls over his shoulder.

"I love you," I call to him as I put the girl's jackets on them. Then I open the front door, and the girls run to the front lawn and wave to him. I blow him a kiss and watch him put his ball cap on as he pedals his old blue bike down the street.

Bill turns, smiles, and waves good-bye.

The girls and I walk to the playground one block away. I think about Bill and what's going on at our greenhouse business. I'll never understand that family, that's for sure. *Lord, wrap Your arms around Bill today, help him to deal with all this stuff going on.*

George is a handsome guy with dark hair and dark eyes. We used to talk and laugh together, but not anymore, not for years. I used to like him, but he changed. His habit has made him thin and gaunt. He gets mad a lot. His friends are creepy. Part of me wants to help him, and I do pray for him; but I have kids in middle and elementary school. I don't want him to influence them; so, we keep our distance.

When George is working at the greenhouse, he doesn't like doing what Bill or Walt, his brothers, need him to do. He wants to work in the office; I guess he wants to be where the money is. They need him to pot plants and set them up in the greenhouse, but he doesn't like to do that. When he pots, he gets mad and stomps off. It's happened before, a lot. Then he doesn't come in for days; and suddenly things are missing. He'll sneak in the greenhouse at night and take plants or tools or whatever he can sell quickly. George needs his drug money. Oh, I can't think about it anymore. It makes me angry, and sad for Bill. *Lord, You know the answer to this one, I don't.*

The stroller goes a-bump, a-bump, a-bump over the sidewalk cracks. I catch up to Abbey at the corner and we cross the street to the playground. The girls swing for a long time. The sky is blue today, and the clouds are white and fluffy. It's a beautiful, cool, spring day.

Thank you for this beautiful day. Bless my Bill with Your strength and wisdom; and give each of us Your peace.

Molly and a Funny Answer to Prayer

1987

Over the past months we have watched our dog Molly's stomach grow pudgy, then round, and then, lately, pumped up like a helium balloon ready to explode. When not pregnant, she is only twenty-two pounds. I think back two years, when I answered an ad in the paper that said, "free puppies." Wendy, Greg, Gavin, Abbey, and I walked across town. Molly was the last puppy they had left, and the runt of the litter. We put Molly in the stroller with Abbey and walked back home. Molly is one of the family now. She has long black fur, a feathery tail, and a brown dot above each eye.

It's late morning. I'm on the floor playing puzzles with our girls, one-year-old Cami and four-year-old Abbey. Bill worked late last night, as he does every Wednesday night. He and his brother Walt run our business. The truck load of plants for Thursday's delivery always gets packed on Wednesday nights. Bill slept late this morning, just finished his breakfast, and went downstairs to the laundry room. I hear the clock strike eleven. Then the laundry room door opens again and closes a few seconds later.

Bill comes up the steps, through the sunny kitchen, to the living room. Standing in the doorway, he holds up one finger to me and mouths the words, "One puppy."

"Oh! Really?" I whisper. I get up quick.

"In the laundry room," he whispers back, motioning with his eyes.

"Girls, let Daddy play puzzles with you," I say as I give him a wooden puzzle piece. I turn and head downstairs.

"Daddy, play wiff uths!" Abbey says.

I go through the kitchen and down the six steps to the laundry room and open the door. Molly's there, in the middle of the small room, licking a tiny black puppy on the floor, chewing the gray afterbirth off him. She grabs the umbilical cord and gnaws it with her teeth, eats it, and then licks the puppy's navel. Puddles of blood and water are on the floor under her. Tiny little legs splay spastically in the air in all directions. Then the puppy slides on the linoleum as Molly roughly turns him over with her tongue and licks the pup all over once more. His little head twists slowly in all directions. His tight shut eyes are directed by his nose to Molly's face. She roughly licks his face too.

"Oh, Molly. He is so cute!" I say. I stoop down and run my hand along Molly's back.

Molly stops, looks at me, and seems to say, "Mom, don't bother me, I have business to do here." Then, she resumes cleaning her pup.

I take a few paper towels and clean up the mess on the floor and put the towels in the trash. I lay a pile of newspapers all over the floor and put some old towels and a soft blanket in the corner right near Molly. I fill her bowl with fresh water. When Molly finishes cleaning the pup, I carefully pick him up. Molly is licking and nuzzling my hands. She yelps at me, following my every move as I hold her pup. Only when I lay the pup back down on the soft blanket does she relax. Then she lies down next to him and licks him some more.

"Oh, Lord, please help my Molly," I pray as I notice her belly is still so big. "Molly, I know how you feel." I pet her small head. *"Lord, help her through this."* Her brown eyes look at me, then look away, then she lays her head down on the blanket, exhausted. The pup nuzzles under her arm and falls asleep. Her fur feels like satin to my touch. "I love you, Mol," I say as I get up, turn, and with one more look, close the door behind me and go upstairs.

Living in a split level, I am always going up and down steps. I go to the living room. Cami dumps a puzzle out on the floor. Bill gets up.

"Dad-dee, 'tay," she says.

"I have to go to work now, Cam." He ruffles her blonde hair, then turns to me and gives me a kiss.

Then, I stop, turn, and grab Bill's arm and whisper, "Hey, what am I going to tell these little ones and the older kids when they ask where puppies come from? Especially the older kids. At thirteen, ten, and seven years old they're bound to be curious . . . though Wendy might be aware. I don't know. They are too young to tell them where puppies come from ..."

Bill shrugs his shoulders, and with a goofy look on his smiling face says, "I dunno, but you'll think of something!"

"Gee, thanks. And where will *you* be?"

"Over the hill and far away," he laughs, "you know, at the salt mines." Bill opens the closet door, pulls his jacket off the hanger, puts it on, and kisses me good-bye.

"Maybe I'll take them to the playground, and then we'll walk over to Carol's." I call to the girls, "Let's get our jackets on and go out."

"I will check on Molly when I get my bike out of the garage. See you tonight," Bill says. He kisses me again and goes downstairs through the laundry room. A minute later, I hear the garage door go up.

"Can Molly come?" Abbey asks me as I put Cami's jacket on her. Oh gosh, what do I tell her? Molly *always* goes with us. *Lord, give me the right words.* "Aah, no, Molly is really tired this morning. Let's leave her home," I say.

Abbey goes to the living room closet, unfazed by my answer. She gets her jacket off the low hook and puts it on, then opens wide the wooden front door and bangs the screen door open.

Outside, Bill closes the garage door, puts on his Phillies baseball cap, and walks his old blue bike around the station wagon. He's brought Abbey's pink Big Wheel and Cami's stroller out of the garage; they're already in the driveway.

"Bye, guys!" Bill says. He swings his leg over the bar of his bike, looks at me and waves, then holds up two fingers. I read his lips, "Two pups." He smiles, then pedals down the street.

Abbey gets on her Big Wheel and rides fast down the sidewalk. I put Cami in the stroller and run to catch up to

Abbey. I wonder about Molly. *Lord, take care of her, and give me an answer if the kids ask where those pups came from.*

I wonder how Molly is doing. I look at my watch and see it is 12:15. I just want to go home and see how she is. But if I wait another hour, the girls will be too tired to think about the dog. Then I can put them in for their nap. We walk to Carol's house.

Carol and I have known each other since Wendy and her daughter Mandy met the first day of kindergarten. She has a son, David, who is a year younger than Mandy. David and Greg play together too. Carol is a great friend. She takes and picks up my kids from school so my girls can nap. I will help Carol paint or watch her kids. She will also give me a perm when I need one. We often have coffee after school, and the kids play together. We laugh a lot.

Carol and I talk while the children play. I tell her about Molly.

"I'm just itching to go home and see her," I say. "But what should I tell the school kids if they ask where the puppies came from? I don't know what to tell them."

Carol smiles and says, "Oh, just tell them they came from the mailman." She laughs hard, and I do too. "They'll be so excited about them they won't even wonder where they came from!" she says, then calls the kids to the table for a sandwich. The girls love to come to Carol's. It's like home to them. We have lunch together and then we get ready to go home.

"I'll pick the kids up from school for you," Carol says.

"That would be great! Thank you so much. I'll see you in a little while," I say.

When the girls are in for their nap, I hurry downstairs to Molly. She lies on the blanket with puppies—lots of them—suckling at her side. I count them. "Seven! Holy cow, Molly!" She wags her tail, as proud as can be.

"Molly, they're beautiful!" I say. I stroke her head, and she sticks out her pink tongue and pants. I think it's a smile. I laugh. ***Lord, thank you, for this little dog and her puppies.*** I pet the warm pups with my finger. I have a thickness in my throat that grabs my breath, the same feeling I get every Sunday when I see the old couple at the end of the pew holding hands. Tender love at its best, it gets me every time. I look away and take a deep breath. It is beautiful, just beautiful, mother and child … or, rather, pups.

Two of the puppies are white with brown markings. They almost look like St. Bernards. The rest are black with brown markings on their face and chest. They all have little pink noses and little pink pads on their feet. I see that three of them are nursing, their paws kneading Molly's belly. They're hungry! The other four are sound asleep, still holding onto Molly. I pet Molly; she lifts her head up, noses my hand, then puts her head down again.

Her water bowl is still full, but the newspapers I laid on the floor are a mess. I gather them up and throw them out. I fill a bucket with some cleaner and mop the laundry room floor. Molly's eyes follow my every move. The "mountain breeze" scent makes the room smell so good.

I leave Molly and go upstairs. I have a little bit of time before the kids come home from school. I sit on the sofa and get my knitting out of the basket. I love to knit. It's so relaxing. I'm working on a green sweater with white airplanes on it for Greg. I immerse myself in the pattern and lose track of time.

A car door opens out front.

Oh boy, the kids are home. I get up and go to the door, which bangs open before I get there. Wendy and Greg burst in.

"Molly had puppies?!" Greg asks.

"Of course she had puppies, she was getting fat," Wendy says, then rolls her eyes at her nine-year-old brother.

"What's that have to do with it?" Greg throws his book bag on the floor.

I open the door for Gavin.

"Molly had puppies? How many? Where is she?" he says.

"In the laundry room," I say. The kids bolt down the steps. I follow them. I'm as excited as they are!

"Carol! We're downstairs!" I call to her as she comes through the front door.

"Don't open the laundry room door yet!" I say.

They all stop, banging into each other.

"Listen, Molly's real tired and the puppies are little, so we can't pick them up right now, and we have to be quiet. Okay?"

Carol's kids crowd the steps too.

Wendy's hand is on the doorknob and it flies open as they all say, "Okay!" and scramble in to see Molly.

"Awww! Look at them!"

"Oohh!"

"Molliee! Look at your puppies!"

"How many are there? One, two, three, four … no, wait, one, two, three, four, five … they keep moving around!"

"Shhhh! Remember what Mom said."

"I get the white one!"

"I like this black one, the big guy!" Greg points, then tucks his hands back behind his back.

"I like them all!

"Can we have one, Mrs. Off?"

"Can we keep them all, Mom?"

I can't believe that Molly is so calm with her new puppies and all these kids. Carol comes down the steps with Abbey and Cami. "I heard Cami upstairs and got her out of her crib, then Abbey woke—ohh, look at the puppies!" Carol says.

"Look at doggieths!" Abbey says. She stoops down and watches them real close.

Molly moves her head and nudges the pups. She gets up first on her front legs, then looks around at the puppies. They slip to the blanket, then she gets up on all four feet. She walks a few steps, then looks back at her puppies.

There's a bang at the back door and Joe, Paul, and Kelley from down the block yell, "Did Molly have puppies?" Their faces are smooshed against the glass storm door. "Wow, we see a lot of them!"

I unlock the back door. "Hold on, guys, let Molly come outside to go to the bathroom," I said. They get out of the way, and Molly slowly walks out the door, across the patio towards the grass. The kids pet her then turn to come inside.

Suddenly, Paul screams, "Eeeeewwww! Look at Molly!!"

All the kids race outside, and I turn.

"Oh my gosh, that's so gross!" Joe shouts, looking close at Molly's up-turned tail.

"What's that?" Greg points to Molly's butt.

The kids are tipped sideways straining to see what's happening. A shot of bloody water splatters the patio. Molly's panting hard.

"Look, something's coming out of her butt!"

"She's pooping, standing up!"

"Oh, my gosh, that's so gross!"

"What's happening to Molly, Mom? Is she all right?" Gavin asks. He grabs my legs.

"It's poop! It's black poop!"

"No, it's not poop," Paul yells, "It has a face! It's a puppy!"

I race over to Molly, and a slippery, wet puppy plops out onto the patio, splaying spastic legs across the cement. Bloody water follows.

"Oh, that's disgusting!"

Molly turns and licks the puppy fast; she licks him all over. She's real rough with him, but he doesn't seem to mind. Molly grabs the umbilical cord and tears it apart.

A chorus of "ewwwwws" echoes all around me.

"Oh my gosh, that's so gross!"

'What's that gray stuff and the string attached to the puppy?"

"Oh, gosh, ewww, Molly's eating it! I can't look."

Molly pushes again and lets out a noisy fart; the afterbirth comes out in a big gush. Molly promptly chews it.

"Ewwww! Why's she doing that? That's just . . . just wrong." Paul swings his arms like he has had enough. But he looks again.

She licks and licks the puppy, then gnaws the placenta again until it's gone.

I feel sorry for Molly and finally say, "Let's bring Molly inside now. You guys can see the puppies tomorrow, okay?" I carefully scoop the tiny puppy up and cradle it against my chest.

"Let's go inside, Molly," I said. She is yelping at my legs and nosing my arms. My kids bang the back screen door open, go inside, and clammer around the pups.

"Wow, wait 'til we tell Mom about this!" I hear Paul say to Kelly and Joe as they go through the gate, "That was better than *Star Wars!*"

As I head inside, I look close at the new life in my hands. This puppy is little and all black. He's my favorite already.

Molly settles with her puppies on the blanket again. She's tired. The kids are still excited, but they go up to the kitchen for something to eat. I put the newest puppy next to its hungry siblings at Molly's side.

In the kitchen, I cut up some apples and pour some juice for the children. They talk about the puppies and Molly, and which one they like best. Carol and I have a hot cup of coffee and laugh again at "the mailman" and good ol' Mol.

When Carol and her children leave, my kids keep checking on Molly and her puppies. After dinner, I let them hold the puppies. I hold the little black one close to my heart.

Thank you, Lord, for helping Molly today, for all these puppies; and, for answering my prayer when I didn't have the words.

The kids never-ever asked me where puppies come from.

Feeding Time, Round One

"Somebody, come and set the table, please," I call over my shoulder, hoping the kids will hear me downstairs in the den.

No one answers.

I lift the lid of the vegetable soup. It smells pretty good. I give it a quick stir with the ladle. The lid slips out of my hand and splashes soup all over the stove. The tomatoey broth splashes on the front of my shirt.

"Oh, phooey!!" I grab a dish cloth and wipe the soup off me making the spot one big smear.

Ugh, dinner. Lord, nothing goes right at dinnertime.

Soup drips from the pot handles. I mop it up. I hear the blare of the television downstairs.

I grab a big colander and drain some noodles from a pot of boiling water. Then, I add them to the vegetable soup. I stir the soup with a big wooden spoon, bang the spoon on the side of the pot, then run it under the spigot for a few seconds.

I call again, "Wendy, Greg, Gavin! Can someone set the table?"

No response, again.

I forget about the soup and head down the short flight of steps to the small den. I hear the whirring of the spinning club chair; it gets louder the closer I get. It's going faster and faster.

"Geg-gie, 'top!" Cami shouts. "'Top! AaaHhh!"

I see Cami spinning around and around in the old club chair, her head plastered against its black and tan brocade velvet sides, blonde hair flying, eyes closed, holding onto Michael, her blanket, for dear life. Greg is lying on the floor, spinning the chair with his feet as fast as he can while he watches the TV, oblivious to her yelling.

"Greg, STOP RIGHT NOW!" I try to grab the edge of the chair, but it spins away.

"Uh-oh," Greg turns his head and sees I'm standing over him with a long wooden spoon. As quick as a flash, he opens his legs and with a great scissor kick, he catches the chair between his legs, and it stops fast. Cami lurches forward and falls out of the spinning chair with a thud to the floor. Her face splats on the ugly gold shag carpet. She lets out an awful scream.

Greg rolls over in a ball of laughter. Wendy and Gavin, who are sitting on the sofa, join him in peals of laughter. Abbey bolts upright from her nap on the other end of the sofa. The spinning chair gets a couple more shoves from Greg's feet as he belly-laughs uncontrollably and thrashes his feet around.

"Greg! Go to your room!" I pick up the screaming toddler. I turn around and point to the others, forgetting I have the spoon in my hand, "and you two, be quiet!"

The other two kids bite their lips. Their cheeks puff out as they try keep their laughs in. The chair whirs slowly to a stop.

"Whoa, that's a big spoon!" Greg says with a laugh. He scooches by me sideways to the hallway steps, like he's crawling over a crowded row in a movie theater.

"Now you got me in trouble, Cam," Greg echoes in the stairwell. Then, a second later, he pops his head back around the doorway from the second step up. He giggles and says, "You doofus, why didn't you hang on, anyway?"

"Because she's a one-year-old, that's why!" I say. "You're nine! She coulda got hurt! You go now!! Upstairs, git!" As I shoo him away, the spoon falls out of my hand and lands on the spinny chair.

I feel tears coming to my eyes. I'm so tired. I wish these kids would be good. Where's Bill when I need him? I wipe the tears from Cami's face, then run my hand through my hair. I haven't brushed it since I got up this morning. I feel like a mess.

I hug Cami, give her Michael, and she slides out of my arms. I step closer to the window to see if Bill is coming. It's almost seven o'clock.

"Uhh, Mom," Gavin says as he cranes his neck sideways. "Can you move? We can't see *Power Rangers*."

I look at him, then turn and snap off the television.

"Ah, Mom, we didn't do anything! It was Greg!" Gavin says. "You're no fun, Mom." He stomps toward the door, picks up a football and slams it to the floor.

"Yeah, Mom, you're no fun," Wendy says joining Gavin by the door.

I look at them. They don't move.

I drop my head; I feel weak all over. "I know. I'm *not* any fun."

I cover my mouth with my fist and look away. I turn to the window and look out at the darkening sky. Then, I whisper, "Please, get out some bowls for soup." I barely heard myself. They leave.

"*You're no fun, Mom*," rings in my ears. I see my reflection in the window. I don't like the person I see. I want to be fun, but there's so much to do at dinner time: get the food ready, spoon out dinner, fill glasses, butter bread, cut up meat. The kids are ornery and hungry ... *and I'm* hungry too! ***There must be a better way to handle this, Lord. But I don't know how to do it by myself. I need Your help.*** A car goes down the street. Its taillights glow red as they turn in the driveway a few houses down.

I turn to go to the kitchen.

Abbey is there behind me, with Bruno, her Cabbage Patch doll, and her green blankie. We look at each other. Then, she takes my hand and says, "I wuv you, Mom-mee. Wet'th doh eat thum thoop."

Feeding Time, Round Two: The Knock-Out

*D*ays later, the words, "You're not any fun, Mom," still haunt me.

It's another day, 8:25 a.m. All faces are washed, teeth brushed, and jackets on. We stop before we go out the door, I say their prayers and kiss them good-bye, the same thing I've done every day since Wendy started kindergarten.

The kids run across the lawn to our blue station wagon in the driveway. The sky is steel gray, the wind whips through overhead wires making strange sounds. Two seagulls squawk as they fight over the top of the telephone pole near the street.

"I get the front seat!" Wendy says. She hip-bumps Greg out of the way and opens the front door.

"Hey, you doofus, watch it!" he says.

"Ha! Too bad," Wendy says. She climbs into the front seat.

"I get up-front on the way home," Gavin says. "Right, Mom?"

As I put Cami in her car seat, I smile and say, "Yeah, Gavin, you can sit up front on the way home." I want to be the fun mom, right?

"You dork," Greg says as he whacks his brother with his lunch bag.

"Mom, Greg hit me!"

The trip to school is only eight blocks long. It seems like ten miles.

I drop the kids off at school. The car is quiet now. From their seats, the little girls look out the windows; raindrops dot the windshield. "You're not any fun, Mom," echoes in my mind again and again. At home, I park the car and get the children in the house before the rain really comes down.

The girls play in the living room. I wash the breakfast dishes, put the cereal boxes away, and start the laundry. I stare out the kitchen window at the rain while I fold clothes. I can't get those words out of my head. I start to cry, then stop myself.

I pick up the receiver of the red phone hanging on the wall and dial my mother's number. Mother always makes me feel good. When I go to her house, she stops everything she's doing. She puts the coffee on—or the tea pot, if it's after four in the afternoon—and we sit at the maple kitchen table in her sunny yellow kitchen and talk. She makes me feel like my visit is the most important part of her day. She does the same when I call. She listens, really listens to me. I wait, the phone rings a few times and then I hear her say, "Hello." I feel better already.

I tell her about the fiasco at dinnertime the other night. She laughs at Greggie's antics. She thinks it's really funny.

"Oh, he's such a hoot!" she says. Then, she laughs away from the phone, which means it's *really, really* funny. I can picture her at her kitchen table throwing her head back in laughter, the gullet in her neck bouncing up and down.

I am not amused.

But ... then, I guess, maybe it *was* funny. I spill out everything else to her and tell her how their words hurt.

"Don't pay any attention to what they say! They're kids!" she says. "But, don't let them control you either! YOU'RE THE MOM! Who cares, if they have to miss their TV program! You're darn right, they should help you. Bill's never there. He's always working. Remember, *you're* the boss. Those kids need you, and if *you* must be tough, then *be* tough! And pray about it. Ask God to give you an answer you could never think of. What is that for a great God like Him to do?"

I hear her talking, but zero in on her mention of Bill. Even though I complain about Bill working all the time, her words about my husband sting. She's right, of course; but, I guess, I think I'm the only one allowed to say it.

Then, she tells me about her job in the school cafeteria. I stretch the curly red phone cord until it's straight out, to reach the box of crayons in the closet for the girls. Mother and I talk about my brothers and laugh some more.

We say good-bye with her last words being, "You're the mom, remember? Don't take any crap from those kids, ya hear me?"

"Yes."

"Good. Love you. Bye."

I hang up the phone and sit down with the girls at the kitchen table. I color a page in their coloring book. They like me to play. I like to color. Magenta is my favorite crayon color, but the point is worn. I peel back the paper a little and color Cinderella's dress. I think about what my mother said. She always puts things into perspective for me. She said to pray about it.

Okay, Lord, I do not know how to handle dinner with these kids. Give me strength and help them to realize I am the mother here. Lord, I need a good answer for this one. Thank you, Lord.

I feel much better already. I'll see how dinner goes tonight.

Macaroni Stew

1 pound elbow macaroni, cooked and drained
2 pounds ground beef, cooked and drained
1 30-oz. can whole tomatoes
3 beef bouillon cubes
3 cups water
1 tbsp. oregano
1 tbsp. basil
2 tbsp. minced onion
2 tbsp. parsley
¼ cup ketchup
2 tbsp. Worcestershire sauce
Salt and pepper

Brown ground beef in deep pot; drain off fat. Add tomatoes, bouillon, and water, bring to a boil. Add remaining ingredients and simmer for 20 minutes. Add cooked macaroni. Stir until blended. Serve topped with mozzarella cheese.

I have made this recipe before. I should know how to make it, but I don't. I read the handwritten card again. I drop the meat into the pot and turn the gas on. I fill another pot with water and set it on the back burner to boil. I search the cupboard for the spices and then crank open the can of tomatoes with my ancient can opener. I'm late getting dinner started. My shoulders are tight; I'm tired. The ragged lid on the can pops up, hanging on by a sliver of metal. I add the tomatoes to the cooked meat, then add the water, bouillon, and Worcestershire too.

After school, I took the boys to baseball practice even though the fields were still wet. I must pick them up soon. I look at the clock now, 5:45; their practice will be over in fifteen minutes. I'll get the girls in the car and pick the boys up. Then I'll swing by and pick Wendy up at her friend's house on the way home. The pot bubbles. It smells good.

The little girls are in the living room with Molly, our dog. Molly barks at something outside. Abbey opens the door to see what's there and Molly bolts out.

"Moll-wie!" Abbey shrieks.

"Oh, no! Molly's out!" I say. "She'll go all over town!"

"Tum back, Moll-wie!" Abbey runs outside after the dog.

I turn off the burners, grab my handbag, scoop Cami up and run out the door. Abbey runs down the sidewalk, but the dog is way down the block.

We all get in the car and search for the dog. We go up and down streets, looking for that little, twenty-five-pound black dog. I scan backyards, porches, and the playground. She's not to be seen. I don't know where she is.

Finally, I turn back towards home, and I see her crossing the street towards Carol's house. I pull up to the curb, shove the car into park, lean over the seat and swing open the front car door.

"Molly! Come here, girl!"

She hears me, comes running, and bounds into the front seat, glad to see us. She hops over the seat to the happy kids. I close the door and head for home. Then, I remember I must pick the others up. I'm late. I turn towards the ballpark.

When we get home, the kids and the dog are all riled up, though Wendy does put the plates on the table before she goes to her room. I scramble to turn on the burners and re-read the recipe and add the remainder of the spices. I set the rest of the table myself, rather than deal with asking the kids. I dump the cooked macaroni into the tomato and meat mixture and stir it around and around. The stew boils. I turn the gas down real low and put the lid on the pot.

I usually have mozzarella cheese with this dish. I open the door of the gold refrigerator and hunt. I thought I had some. I move the milk and iced tea around, look in the crisper drawer. It should be somewhere in here. I see a small block of cheese in the back of the drawer. Yuck, I don't even know what it is. It's all green and gross. I heave it into the trash can. I guess I don't have any mozzarella. Oh, well, no cheese tonight.

I grab two potholders and lift the big cast iron pot of macaroni stew to the hot pad on the table.

I call the kids, and to my surprise they all come at once. The dog is barking for her food. Greg gives Molly a scoop of dry food and shoves her bowl and the container of food across the floor. I use the old can opener and start to crank open a big can of dog food. Greg goes to his chair, hooks his foot around the rungs and stops dead.

"Not this slop again!" he says.

The other kids look in the pot.

"Uhh-gh! That stuff's the worst."

"Oh, no, not this."

"I hate that stuff. I'm not eating."

"Yucky 'tuf!"

"Where's the cheese? I don't see any. It's rotten without the cheese. I'm not eatin' that."

I turn the stupid can opener with such force, the lid flies off and onto the floor. I put the dog food on the counter, then I go quietly to the table and take the big black pot back to the stove. I don't say a word; the kids grow silent.

I pick up the can of dog food.

"If you don't like what I cook," then I explode, "**you can eat this!**" I slam the dog food can down on the table and throw a serving spoon into it. The spoon stands straight up in the brown, lumpy mush.

"Nooooo, Momm-iiieee."

"No, we'll eat the other stuff!"

"Waaaaahhhhh!"

"Aahh, come on, Mom!"

"**Oh, you don't like that either? Then, maybe you'd like some of this?**" I grab the plastic container of dry dog food and march around the table slamming handfuls of dry food on each plate.

"Mommy, we're sorry. We'll eat!"

"Mom, I really like that tomatoey junk."

"Mommmm, pleaseeee, we'll eat!"

"**You're darn tootin', you'll eat! This is your dinner! So eat! I'm not taking any more crap from you kids at dinner, EVER! Do you hear me??!! Never again! You'll all sit here**

until you're done. And don't go begging to Daddy when he decides to walk in!"

"What's the matter here?" Bill says from behind me.

"What's the matter? What's the matter? Why, it's *feeding time* **at the zoo! THAT'S what's the matter!"**

"She gave us dog food!"

"Yeah, DOG FOOD!"

"Yucky 'tuf!"

I look at Bill, and I must have scared him.

"Why don't you go out for a while, dear. I'll deal with these guys," he says. He puts his arm around my shoulder, but I shrug him away.

"They will eat dog food for dinner or go to bed without it! Is that clear?" I spit the words through my teeth. "They will be good at dinner from now on," then I add, "and YOU TOO!" I stare at his wide-open blue eyes.

"Yes, they … er … WE will," he says.

I am in tears, and so tired.

"Won't you, kids? Huh?" he says. I see him wiggle his fingers at them for a response.

I see five nods. Bill takes my shoulders and turns me towards the living room door. I grab my purse and leave without looking back.

I have never been as mad as I was that night. I went to Burger King for dinner. I had a hamburger with extra pickle, mustard, onions, and ketchup, fries, and a diet Coke. I sat at a booth near a window overlooking the street. Just me, alone; it was quiet and peaceful. It felt like a little bit of heaven. I sipped my soda slowly and watched a family with some kids carry their tray away from the counter. Thankfully, they went to the back of the dining room. I stayed at that little booth until the sun went down behind the hardware store across the street. It was great. Fries never tasted so good. I gathered my wrappers and stuffed them in my empty cup.

I don't know what made me get so mad. I have never ever screamed like that. It was as if someone else was doing the screaming instead of me. Could that be possible? Oh, who knows; only, just maybe, the kids got the message this time.

*   *   *

But, after that night, the kids were good at dinner. I never again had a problem with them at a meal. God did answer my prayers in a way I never dreamed of. He didn't give me the *good* answer I asked for: He gave me a *great* answer.

Dogs in Heaven

*B*ill's mom, Elizabeth, and I disagree on one thing: where dogs go when they die. I say they go to heaven. She says she has never read that in the Bible. I *know* that the dogs I have had are in heaven. God has lions and lambs in heaven—the Bible says that. He thought animals were important enough that Noah had to save them. She still disagrees ... and then we laugh together! Someday we will both find out which one of us is right.

*   *   *

Molly was with us for twelve years. Losing a pet is never easy. My heart slowly broke one winter.

I loved to lie on the floor in the early afternoons and read books for the class I was enrolled in at the local community college. I especially loved to put my book in the patch of sunlight coming through the large living room window. I would read and move the textbook as the sunlight moved across the floor. Molly would lie next to me. I would stroke her head and rub her belly. One day, I found a lump on her tummy. Her brown eyes watched me as I felt the bulge. My heart sank.

I take Molly to the vet. She has breast cancer, but the doctor says she can operate. We schedule a date for the beginning of January.

"Is Molly going to die?" Cami asks.

"Well, the doctor will operate on her and take the tumor out," I say, trying to sound optimistic. But, I think to myself … Molly *is* twelve years old.

"Mommy, I love her!" Cami starts to cry. She cuddles with Molly on the floor. "I don't want to go to school tomorrow. I want to be with Molly."

It is our son, Gavin, who loves Molly most, though. He's seventeen now. He was six when she had all those puppies. He fed her. He walked her. Molly slept with him. When Molly ran away, he's the one who would ride all over the neighborhood on his bike, leash wrapped around his handlebars, looking for her. The older kids would be busy with homework, and the younger ones couldn't cross any streets. Gavin would take charge and always came back riding his bike with her on the leash prancing beside him.

So, Bill, Gavin, Abbey, Cami, and I give Molly the royal treatment. (Wendy and Greg are away at college.) She loves the attention.

The day comes for her surgery. I arrive early and the technician takes Molly to be prepped. I fill out paperwork in the waiting room. I turn to leave. The doctor comes out from the surgery room.

"Debby, I just looked at Molly. I'm sorry, but I can't operate on her. The tumor has metastasized. It's inoperable now." She comes closer. "It's grown too big, too fast. I am sorry," she says as she spreads her hands out wide.

"You're sorry …" I try to understand her. "I thought you were going to help her today?"

"The cancer is too far gone. The best you can do now is to make her comfortable and keep her to her regular routine until—"

"—Until we have to put her down?" I stare wide-eyed at her.

"Yes. I can't do anything else for her." She shakes her head.

I know in my heart Molly's going to die. But hearing Dr. D. say it just makes it too final. Besides, what do I tell the children when they get home from school or my other kids when I call them at college?

The technician brings Molly out to the waiting room. Her whole belly is shaved bare. The tumor protrudes through her pink skin out the left side of her belly. I look away. I have a big clump in my throat. It must be my heart.

"Call me if you need me, Debby," the doctor says. She hands me the leash and pats my arm.

I look at Molly, shaved belly and all. She hangs her tongue out and looks like she's smiling. I smile, the clump moves. I say, "Thank you, Dr. D. I appreciate your honesty."

*   *   *

Molly is failing. She gets out of breath a lot, but her appetite is good. She still wants to go get the children from school with me. I must lift her into the car though. It will be soon, I tell myself.

Gavin takes a Monday and Tuesday off from school in February. He's going with Bill in a big Ryder truck, full of plants and supplies, to a grower in Virginia. They will stay at Greg's dorm at the University of Virginia that night and come home on Tuesday.

The night before Bill and Gavin leave, Molly is really bad. She's exhausted. She sits on the carpet, legs splayed out in front supporting her massive belly. She cannot lie down. If she lies down the tumor crushes her lungs, and she can't breathe. She is panting hard. I have been with her all night. It is now 2 a.m. She's so tired she starts to fall over, then she wakes up panting hard for air. I sit on the floor and hug her, leaning her little head on my shoulder so she has a support and a pillow. I brace her front legs with my folded ones. I hear the clock strike three.

Gavin comes downstairs and takes my place as Molly's bolster. I curl up on the sofa and pull the afghan over me. I listen to her every breath. I see them together. I see her eyes close; I close mine too.

Lord, I must put her down. She can't go on like this. Dogs are supposed to go to a dark corner and die, aren't they? I don't know if I can do this.

Molly sleeps, breathing hard, then wakes. Gavin moves his legs to a different position.

I wake and hear the clock strike five. Molly struggles to walk. She doesn't want any water. She hasn't eaten in two days. I get up and kneel beside her. Gavin puts his arm around me. Her breath is hot. Oh, Molly, this isn't fair to you. I cry into her soft black coat and want the night to end, yet not this little life.

At six o'clock, Bill has the truck ready to go. Through the frosty window, I see Bill loading two gym bags behind the front seat. He looks at his watch.

I stop Gavin by the front door as he gets his coat on. I look at his blue eyes and whisper, "Gavin, thank you for staying with me last night. But you have to say good-bye to Molly before you go. She can't breathe. It's time." I see his pain; he's losing his friend. He hugs me tight for a long time. My shoulder is wet from his tears. The front of his shirt is wet from mine.

"I know," he says. "I can't watch her suffer, Mom," he wipes his eyes with the heel of his hand, then straightens. "You do what you have to do. I just don't want to be there when you do. She's my best friend." Gavin looks away, then turns and goes into the den to Molly.

I can't look. *Lord, how do I put this dog down? How do I do this, Lord? In olden days they used to shoot sick dogs out behind the barn. I always thought that was a horrible thing to do. Now, I must do the exact same thing, but without a gun. I am no different than them! This dog has given us such joy, Lord . . . help me, please!*

Bill comes inside. "Gavin, we have to get going to beat the traffic in Washington, D.C." He looks at me, then he goes in to see Molly.

"Hey, old girl, you're the best pup, ya know. We don't like to see you hurting."

Molly pants, then her legs buckle.

"Can't you stay and go with me, Bill?"

"I can't, Debby. I would if I could," he says. I see tears in his eyes.

I look away and go to the kitchen. The thought of coffee or breakfast makes me sick.

Bill follows me and kisses me good-bye. I feel numb, and alone. I say my prayers with Gavin, as we always do, and I pray for our dog; but my prayers are a struggled whisper. Gavin hugs me for a long while, then crosses the front lawn and gets in the truck without looking back.

At eight o'clock I call Dr. D., and she says to bring Molly over this morning. Molly walks slowly to the car, taking her time. Then I hoist her in. I take the girls to school and they each hug Molly good-bye.

I can't do this.

I go back to the house. I call my mother.

"Debby, you have to put her down," Mother says. "She's suffering! No one wants to suffer. Life is no fun for her. Besides, she's waiting to *not* be in pain. She's been a good dog. Now it's time for her to go to doggie heaven."

Molly died at ten that morning. My two nieces, Beth Anne and Amy, took off from work and went to the vet with me. We hugged each other and cried in the hallway for a long time. I wasn't alone, and Molly wasn't in pain anymore. Beth Anne and Amy helped me carry Molly to the car in the shallow cardboard box the vet gave me to bring her home. When I peeked in the box, Molly wasn't struggling anymore. She even had a smile on her face.

Lord, thank you for taking care of our great little pup. I think she likes heaven.

The Three Old Swimmers

*T*here's not a parking spot to be found along any of the streets near the Waverly Road beach in Ocean City, New Jersey. All the "shoobies" come down from Philadelphia on Saturdays, especially when the week has been hot. ("Shoobies" got their name decades ago, because people who came to the shore for the day brought their lunch in shoeboxes.) All this July has been unbearably hot. Today is supposed to be our weekly fun time together, and I can't find a place to park. I drive on.

"Mom-mee, there'th a parkin' thpot!" Abbey says. She points to the opposite side of the street.

I make a three-point turn into a narrow driveway and head the other way. I wave another driver on and motion to him that I'm taking that space. I finagle the car into the spot, and the girls get their buckets and shovels.

Then, I see the parking meter.

"Ugh, phooey."

Lord, I just want to go to the beach with the girls. Help me find some kinda change please. I never have money when I need it.

I search my handbag. Nothing.

I look in the glove compartment. Nothing.

"Tan we dit out, Mom? It'th dittin' hot en here," Abbey says.

"I know it's real hot in here," I say, "but I have to find some change." I slide my hand under the seat and find a quarter. I look under the passenger seat and see a dime.

"Thank you, Lord!" I say.

"Okay, I found some money! Let's go!"

I lift Abbey up and she puts the money in the meter and turns the little dial. She laughs.

We did find a place to park, but we're three blocks from the beach. Three blocks with a six-year-old and a three-year-old is a long way. Abbey walks a few feet ahead. I hold Cami's hand and carry the beach bag in one hand and my chair in the other. I feel the sweat drip down the center of my back. Four o'clock is the hottest time of the day. The girls try not to step on the sidewalk cracks. Cami's sandal comes off. I fix it for her. A few steps later, the other one comes loose. I bend and put that one back on her foot.

Abbey says, "Mom, tum on, let'th go."

"I'm tryin'."

We finally get to the beach and walk over the dunes. The sun is beginning its descent; it sheds a soft light over the sand. The girls run toward the water, then plop down on the sand and dig with their shovels. I open my sand chair and collapse into it. I'm exhausted. The girls run in the water then come back with their buckets full, splashing water along the way.

"Mom-mee p'ay wiff uth!" Abbey says.

"I will in a few minutes, okay?" I watch them play. They dump their buckets, and the water disappears into the sand. I see them, but my thoughts are on different things. I bite my lip; tears are pooling behind my eyes. I look away.

"Lord, I'm just struggling. I don't understand how what I do is important. I just do mundane things, everyday things to keep this house running and our family going. This morning, I drove Wendy, Greg, and Gavin to their cousin's house, came home and mowed the front lawn, did laundry, picked some tomatoes, made lunch, did the dishes, and played Barbies. I love my family, Lord, and taking care of our home. I'm happy, but my entire day is spent doing stuff like that. You know the line in the old hymn that goes, "Make me a blessing to someone today"? Well, Lord, I just don't get it. How can I make a difference to anyone when I'm busy doing simple stuff all day?

I get up from my chair and walk to Abbey and Cami at the water's edge. They fill their buckets with sand and turn them over with a thump. They giggle as they lift the buckets away, then stop short when the ocean swirls around their lopsided castles and melts them into the sea. Then they laugh again, and I do too. Water droplets glisten on their sun-kissed skin.

I sit down and dig into the wet sand with both hands. I remember this same feeling of sand under my fingernails and the smell of the ocean from when I was a child. My parents would rent a place here in Ocean City at 18th Street. I loved it here. I still do. The water washes against my legs. I watch the girls dig a shallow moat around another try at a sandcastle.

I turn my head and look toward the dunes and stop.

I see three old ladies. They are making their way over the sand dunes slowly, very slowly, with arms linked. Each one is in a bathing suit from years ago, their pale skin a sharp contrast to the old black suits. Each lady is hunched over and wary of her steps, and yet determined to get to the beach.

What catches my eye, though, is the one in the middle: she is small and frail. She hangs on to her friends with both arms and gauges her every step across the uneven sand. This small central figure, although old and bent, beams as she teeters side to side. I can see her smile, even though her face is silhouetted against the pink sky. But what tickles me most is that she has on a white swimmer's cap.

I watch them for a long time, and finally the trio reaches the water. Then, it dawns on me. The old ladies are helping this beloved friend across the beach, so she can put her feet in the water.

I have a lump in my throat, but I can't look away.

I see joy and exhilaration on their faces as the shallow ocean waves lap against their feet. Their laughter is muffled in the breeze. I wrap my arms around my knees, swish my feet across the sand. I smile and watch, mesmerized by them. The three need each other for support; they hold on tight. They laugh into the wind. They never let go. Tears sting my eyes for the second time today, this time for a different reason.

I see them gaze out to sea. They smile and watch the waves swirl through their legs. I hear their windswept voices and giggles again and again. They remain in the water, arms linked, for a long time, but never do they get wet past their knees. Finally, they turn around and help their loved one and each other, slowly, very slowly, step by step, across the shadowed sand, then up and over the dunes toward the peach-colored sun.

I swallow that lump in my throat as I watch them disappear out of sight. What a tremendous, yet simple, act of love. Yes, a simple act of love.

"Oh, no! The cath-thle ith meltin'!!"

Their sandcastle topples into the moat, then disappears.

"It'th gone!" Abbey shrieks, then she and Cami, with buckets in hand, both prance and frolic around the moat, splashing me too! "Oh," I say, laughing. My thoughts are suddenly renewed! They ping pong back and forth from the old swimmers to the beautiful children God has given to me.

My heart is renewed.

Yes, Lord! Everything I do for these kids and our family; I do it with great love—just like that trio over the dunes. That is the blessing I give to others!

Now I get it, Lord.

I smile, turn, and look at Cami and Abbey. My heart soars with love for them and I feel a great peace come over me.

The tide is coming in.

"Let's build another castle," I say, as I fill a bucket, pound the sand down, and flip it over. Twice more I repeat that. Three castles must be stronger than one! Then, we drizzle wet sand through our fingers and make "drippy drop" turrets on top of them. They look perfect!

"Here tumth dah wave-th!" Abbey yells as a big wave crashes over top of our triple castle; then another wave, and another comes. In the blink of an eye our hard work is now just another flat part of the watery beach. Everything is gone.

We are wet and covered with sand. The water ebbs back into the ocean, then we look at each other, and start to laugh. The girls look at me with their blonde hair blowing in the wind, and their happy, sand-dusted faces lifted towards the sky. I know then that I am the luckiest person in the world.

"Let's go in the water!" I say. I pick up a squealing Cami and run into the waves. Abbey catches up and belly flops into the water next to us. I smile and laugh out loud and see the joy on their faces. We splash and jump waves for a long time; until the sun goes down below the dunes.

Later, we drag our feet through the shallow waves and the girls gather their buckets and shovels. I fold up the beach chair and put the wet towels in my bag. We plod over the dunes; the sand is cool on our bare feet. I smile all the way to the car. What a great day it has been.

Oh Lord, thank you for showing me what I didn't understand.

The things that I do are important, because I do them with love for my Bill and our children. Being busy sometimes makes me forget the reason why I do what I do.

Yes, the simple things I do, like driving kids to a friend's house, building sandcastles, or even taking them to the beach so they can put their feet in the ocean—these things done with love are the blessings that mean the most.

A Mother's Love:
The Ups and Downs

"Wendy, how about this? This is so cute!" I say as I hold up a shirt in the junior department of J.C. Penney.

"Mom, it's yellow. I don't do yellow," Wendy says as she stands next to me. She rolls her eyes.

"Then, look for something you like, Wendy. I don't know what you like. I'm just trying to help you. There are tons of clothes here," I say.

Wendy crosses her arms. "I don't want to," she says.

"I know you don't," I say with a sigh.

Oh no, Lord, not again. How can a fourteen-year-old not care about clothes? I need Your help, Lord. Help me and give me patience with this girl. Lord, now that I've started to work part-time with Bill at the greenhouses, I finally have some extra money to spend, and I want to treat her to something new. Is there something wrong with that, Lord? Wendy always looks neat, but I know she needs some new things. She never complains, though. I guess I just want to honor her. Is that strange? Can't a mother do that, Lord? Or is buying new clothes just a parent's duty? She's my right arm with the younger children. She helps me all the time. I just want to do something nice for her. Am I wrong?

"Come on, Wendy, there are all kinds of styles, anything you want!" I say, and smile at her.

"I don't like clothes shopping, and you know it."

I bristle, then turn and face her. "Well, you had better choose something or I will buy what I think you would look great in, including that yellow shirt. Besides, you need some new things now because you refused to look for clothes when you started school in the fall. You want to look nice, don't you?" I raise my arms in despair.

"I *do* look nice. I just don't like to shop, and I wouldn't wear that yellow shirt if you bought it for me!"

"Then, you'd better pick something out." I snap back and turn away.

Wendy turns and flips through the shirts, zinging the hangers across the bar faster than a bullet. She grabs a black shirt and a green one, then stomps away to look at some jeans.

"Geggie, 'top!" Cami yells.

I see Cami holding on to Michael, her blanket, for dear life. Cami named her blanket Michael almost as soon as she could talk. I don't know why she picked that name or why in the world she wanted to name her blanket, but it stuck. So, her yellow waffle-weave blanket's name has always been Michael

Cami is in her Umbroller stroller and Greg is pushing it around the racks of clothes like he's at the Indy 500.

"Not so fast, Greg!" I say.

"Ah, Mom. She likes it. Don't you, Cam?" He stops the stroller but gives her little butt a boot with his foot.

"Geggie! 'top!"

"Stop what, Cam?" Greg says as he holds his arms out to the side. He laughs like a hyena, with a grin that will surely make him grow horns.

Abbey is sitting with Bruno, her Cabbage Patch doll, on the dais next to a mannequin in a tie-dyed dress. Gavin is standing next to her, looking closely at the mannequin's face.

"She's creepy," Gavin says.

Abbey looks up at the girl, "Thee'th not kweepy. Thee'th boootiful!"

"Yeah, right, Abs!" Gavin says. He leaps off the platform.

"Gavin, behave! You're in a store, not at home," I say. I should have left the kids at home, but I couldn't find anyone to watch them. Hopefully, we'll get a shirt or two and get home quick.

"Wendy, since you found two shirts and a pair of jeans, why don't you at least try those on?" I say.

"I have to TRY THEM ON?" Wendy shrieks. Her green eyes throw daggers at me.

"Yes, you do," I say.

"Do you like thith thkirt, Wen-ny?" Abbey asks. She holds up a pair of pink print culottes. "It'th tho pretty!"

"I don't do skirts, Abs. And I don't do pink! Go play with Bruno."

"Wendy, she's just trying to help. What's with you, anyway?" I say. I spin around to her. "Go in and try those things on, please."

Wendy tromps off to the fitting room.

I take a deep breath. My palms are sweaty, and my teeth are clenched. ***Lord, it's hard shopping with these children. But . . . I can do this. I'm really trying my best.***

I look through some racks of clothes. My mind goes to thoughts of Bill at work. I'm glad I'm not there today. There is sure to be fireworks after last night.

Bill was working late at Uncle Lou's greenhouse. He has been "moonlighting" for Uncle Lou's business a few nights a week for a few years now, to make some extra money. Bill was potting orchid plants there late last night and he heard some noise in the packing room. He peeked through the window of the door and saw his brother, George, taking a ladder and some tools. Bill caught him as he was going out the front door.

"George, what are you doing?" Bill shouted.

Startled, George stammered, "Err, my friend has to fix something."

"At midnight? Here?" Bill yelled. "You don't belong here! And those things don't belong to you! Get out!"

George left. Bill called Uncle Lou. Lou knew that George was trouble. Like a snake, he could squeeze into any place, at any time. Alarm systems were nothing to him.

Lou called the cops.

When Bill goes to work today his family won't be happy. They always defend George, no matter what he does. Bill tells them they are wrong. They tell Bill they have faith that their prayers for George are being answered, and that Bill should have more compassion for his brother.

It's just unbelievable.

"Lord, take care of my Bill today. Give him the strength he needs to stand up for what is right.

Before I move to the next rack of clothes I count heads. One, two, three … where's Gavin?

I scan the racks of clothes and suddenly his head pops up in the middle of a circular rack of bikinis.

"You, dweeb!" Greg says, as he laughs and does a few 360s with the stroller. Cami closes her eyes and holds the sides of the stroller tight as she whirls around fast in circles.

"Geggie! Michael!!" Cami shouts as her blanket flies out of her hands.

Greg snatches Michael from the floor, rolls "him" into a football, and hurls him to Gavin as he comes out from under the bathing suits. Gavin catches the blanket and runs down the aisle, stuffing Michael into the seat of his pants. Abbey laughs and runs after Gavin.

"Michael's a butt-wadd!!" Greg shouts and howls with laughter, spinning Cami around and around in the Umbroller.

"No! Gimme 'im!" Cami shouts.

"Michael'th a butt-wadd," Abbey chimes in and laughs.

"No," Gavin shouts, "he's not butt-wadd Michael. He's 'Butt-Sniffing *Larry Appleton!'* He struts around swinging his backside like one big hot mama. Gavin claims that if Cami can name her blanket, he can give "him" a name too. So, he calls her blanket, "Larry Appleton" the name of his favorite character in a TV sit-com.

"Gavin, 'top! Mommieee!" Cami wrestles with her lap belt, trying to undo it.

"Boys, behave!" I shout and turn to go after them, trying to rescue Michael.

Gavin darts away from my grab. He whips Michael out of his pants and swirls the blanket around his forehead and ties it in a knot behind his head.

"Now, he's 'Doo-rag Larry Appleton!'" Gavin says, as he tosses his head side to side and points his arms straight up and then straight down snapping his fingers to an unheard beat. He hip-hops to the right and then to the left.

"Go! You go, Doo-Rag Larry!" Greg yells, whirling Cami around again in the stroller.

"MOM!!! Come here!" Wendy yells.

"Oh, brother," I rub my head and head to the fitting room. I grab the stroller from Greg.

"Gavin, give Michael back!" I call behind me. I leave Cami in the stroller at the side of the fitting room door and go in. Wendy throws open the cubicle door. She has on a green shirt that's miles too big.

"Wendy, that doesn't fit."

"Humph," she spits out, then slams the door closed.

"Try on the black one and the jeans. See how they look," I say more politely than I feel. I go out of the fitting room. *Lord, I'm at my wits end.* I see the boys tossing Michael back and forth. They're finally being good and they're quiet. *Thank you, Lord.* Abbey is walking Bruno, her Cabbage Patch doll, in the stroller.

"Hey, WHERE'S CAMI?"

I look around. I don't see her anywhere. I crane my neck and look all around. I stoop down and look under the clothes racks; maybe she's hiding? She's not there either. Where can she be? I just left her for a second.

"Where's Cami?" I shout to the kids. "Where is she? Why weren't you watching her?" I yell.

"I dunno. I didn't know we had to," Greg says. He and the other kids give me wide-eyed goofy looks.

"Greg, you and Gavin go and look up that way," I say as I point to the men's department. I don't see any salespeople around. I don't even see any customers. The store seems deserted. It's weird. I don't like this feeling I have. *Lord, please help us find Cami. Lord, she has to be here somewhere. Lord, what could she be doing? She couldn't have gone far, unless* … I think of thoughts no parent wants to think. *No, Lord, You are with her. Please help me find her.*

"Cami, where are you?" Wendy shouts as she runs over to me. "Don't worry, Mom, we'll find her." She pats my back then heads down a different aisle.

"Cami!" I yell. I hear the kids calling her name, too.

I imagine Cami's picture on the side of a milk carton or stapled to telephone poles all over New Jersey. *Lord, take these thoughts away. I know You are with her.*

Wendy, Abbey, and I run toward the center of the store where the jewelry department and perfume counters surround the escalators. There is no one around there either. Five o'clock in the afternoon and no one here? It's just spooky. The boys come running to us. "We didn't find her!" Greg says.

We all call her name again.

Suddenly, a voice yells back to us, "Hey, are you looking for HER?"

I look up the length of the escalator to the second floor and there is a woman holding a crying Cami up in the air!

"Yes!" I scream. "That's her!" I can't run up the moving escalator fast enough to reach my baby. I grab Cami out of the lady's arms and hold her tight. "Oh, thank you, thank you," I say to the lady.

"She was just wandering around up here," the lady says. "Then, I heard you calling her."

"Thank you so much!" I say again, and again, as the rest of the kids trip off the escalator steps.

"Yo, Cam, you doofus, where'd you go?" Greg says and smiles. He pats her butt.

"Yeah," Gavin says. "Doo-Rag Larry Appleton didn't know where you were." He shoves Michael into her arms. She buries her head in Michael's yellow softness.

"Cami, you scared us!" Wendy says.

"Yeth, yu thkared uth," Abbey says.

Thank you, Lord, for finding Cami. Thank you for this lady, for hearing me call out to You, and for these kids. I'm just so tired, Lord. I just want to go home now. All of us just want to go home.

*   *   *

That night we eat spaghetti for dinner in our dining room. We tell Bill the story of Cami getting lost. He smiles and laughs.

"Bill, it was scary," I say. "I didn't know where she was." I look at his blue eyes.

"I know, it must have been terrifying," he says and then smiles again. "But everything's fine now." He reaches across the corner of the table and holds my hand. The kids leave the table and head for the den. I hear their plates clatter into the sink.

"What happened at work today?" I ask Bill. His hand is warm; I rub my thumb over his worn gold wedding ring.

"The police came and arrested George," he says. He looks out the window at the darkness. "The family is upset. They don't think I should have ratted on George and called Uncle Lou. Debby, I saw him stealing ladders and tools from Lou's greenhouse when I was working there last night! I told him to get out! I *had to* call Uncle Lou!"

"Oh, brother, I love your family, but I'll never understand them," I say as I roll my eyes. I get up, give him a kiss and hug him tight. "Just last month Uncle Lou's three hundred pound safe was stolen. Then the next day, George brings Lou the insurance papers from inside the safe claiming he found them blowing around outside. George was the good guy then, because he returned them."

"We knew he stole the safe, but we couldn't prove it."

"You're the one who's right in this," I whisper in his ear. "Uncle Lou is right too. You did the right thing. Georgie must be stopped."

Then, I stand up straight and fling my arms out wide and ask, "Why do they always defend George, your mom especially?" The flame of the centerpiece candle bends and flickers.

Bill looks at me and he says, "Her faith in God is very strong, you know that. She has been praying for George for many years. She is acting out her faith—that he's an honest guy, that her prayers for his healing are answered, and that he's not a crook. Besides, he's her son."

"So are you," I say and look into his sad eyes.

Only the tick of the big clock on the wall cuts the silence.

"I know," he finally whispers. He puts his hand on top of mine and laces our fingers together. We look at each other and sigh together.

"I guess we've both had a busy day," I say. I smile at him.

He smiles back and says, "Yes, we have."

An hour later, I pour myself a cup of tea. I take it to the dining room and sit alone. I notice the white tablecloth has orange spaghetti stains on it. I smile and don't care one bit. I look out the window at the darkness. The mellow shades of orange, red, yellow, and green of the hanging Tiffany lamp and the double rows of empty Windsor chairs around the table reflect in the glass panes. It's quiet now. I think about the afternoon. I think about shopping and then about Bill and that fiasco.

Thank you, Lord, so much, for being with us today. We need Your help and Your strength to do what's right and serve You, no matter what. There's a lot we'll never understand, Lord, but I know You are with us.

Cami comes into the dining room dragging Michael behind her.

I smile and lift her onto my lap. She lays her head on my chest and pops her thumb into her mouth. I run my hand over her head and through her soft blonde hair.

"Cami, you really scared Mommy today. I didn't know where you were. Why did you go up those moving steps?"

Cami takes her thumb out of her mouth. Suddenly, she turns and looks at me and says, "Mommy, I diddin' doh up da 'teps, I wen' tup da wailing."

"What?!!" I shout. The hair on the back of my neck stands up straight. "You went up the railing!"

"Yeah, on me tummy!" Cami says with a nod of her blonde head. She sticks her thumb back in her mouth and snuggles against me again. She fingers the satin edge of Michael.

I look up to the ceiling and close my eyes. I picture her standing at the foot of the escalator, feeling the railing move quickly over her fingers. (I'd seen my other kids do that.) Then, suddenly she grabs the sides of the railing . . . and up she goes! To one side of the railing are the escalator steps, and to the other side a sheer drop to the perfume counter below.

Oh, Lord, sometimes it's a good thing not knowing what your kids are doing.

A Whiskey Bottle, a Tackle Box, and Some Pigs

I *like change. Not the kind that comes when you move to a new house or go to a new school, but change, as in pennies, nickels, dimes, and quarters. I started out as a young numismatist, a collector of coins, but now I simply have an obsession to save them. I love coin banks. I have lots of them. Coins have played a big part in my life since I was a little girl living on Arbor Road, in Cheltenham, Pennsylvania.*

My husband and I have lived in our house in Somers Point, New Jersey, for more than thirty-five years. We raised our five children here, and now we enjoy having this big house all to ourselves. Our children are all living on their own. They're working and happy. But now, I am determined to clean out some of the things we've collected in our house.

I stand on a small stool in front of the tall chest of drawers, an antique highboy. It stands on Queen Anne legs, and has eleven drawers, and a pinnacle top that almost reaches the ceiling in the living room.

I wobble on the small stool then balance myself. My right arm reaches over the front of the highest drawer, while I grab the nearby wall with my left hand. I'm on tiptoes, my feet barely touching the stool. I peek over the edge of the drawer and root under papers, ledger books, old 45 records, crocheted doilies, wool hats, and old maps. I toss some of the stuff on the floor.

The stale smell of the drawer reminds me of the drawer where my mother kept everything from wrapping paper to mittens when I was a kid. Then, I see some old coin folders. I had forgotten about them. I pull one out of the drawer. Its edges are worn, and pale green mildew on one corner of the front cover forms a pattern like fine lace.

As I shove the drawer closed and get down off the stool, I finger the circle imprints on the front and back covers of the old coin folder. I wipe off some of the mildew with my sleeve. "Buffalo Nickel Collection 1913–1938" is printed in small silver letters on the front cover of the faded blue book.

*   *   *

I am seven years old again. It is 1960. I am at home on Arbor Road.

Scottie, my nineteen-year-old brother, shakes a two-gallon whiskey bottle up and down over the dining room table. I hold my ears as cold hard cash hits the glass top of the round wooden table. So much money! Coins roll, fall flat, mound up, and slide down again and again. I snatch up some fallen money on the floor like mom's new Hoover vacuum.

"Gimme back my money, you dipshit! Then beat it! Scram!" Scottie yells. He steadies the hanging lamp he had whacked with the bottle by accident.

I throw the coins on the table, lock my hands behind my back, and stare at Scottie. Mommy doesn't like it when he calls me that name. She says it's a bad word, a word Jesus doesn't like; but Scottie doesn't care.

He drops the empty bottle on the floor and smooths the coins out all over the table with his large hands, under the moving shadows of the light. Then he takes each coin and looks at it front and back.

Curiosity makes me stay. He realizes I won't go away.

"Come here, dipshit, I wanna show ya something," he calls me with a jerk of the raised thumb of his gigantic fist under the still swaying lamp.

Slowly, I walk around the table, keeping my hands linked. He sits down in the dining room chair, his eyes still scanning the coins. I stand close to his chair, so close I smell the Old Spice aftershave on his face, and the motor oil smeared on the front of his plaid shirt.

"Look at this penny. It has a date stamped right here." He points to the bottom of the coin. I lean closer to see.

"That's the year it was made." He smooths his hand over the table of coins and picks another penny up. "When was this one made?"

I lean over to get a better look. The swirls of Scottie's fingers are imbedded with dark grease from working on his old blue jalopy.

"Get your head out of the light, dipshit!"

I move my head to the left. "1953," I say. I smile as I take the penny and look at it real close. "Who's the guy?"

"Abe Lincoln; he was a president."

"Oh."

"Now," Scottie hunches closer to me. His face is so close I can see the pores his black whiskers come out of. "Below the date is a letter 'D.' That's for Denver, the city where it was made. Sometimes the letter is on the front and sometimes it's on the back of the coin."

"Wow, that's keen." I say. I sift through some of the coins near me. I look at another penny. "What's an 'S' for?"

"Sacramento, but they don't make money there anymore. They closed that mint down."

"What's a mint?" I ask, wondering how he gets his hair to stand up straight in the front.

"It's the place where they make money, dipshit. Whaddya think?"

"Oh," I say. "I dunno." I look at my hands. He called me that name again.

"Here's a nickel with a 'P' for Philadelphia printed on the back of it."

I look at him. I look at the nickel. He searches the coins.

"How come it's not an 'F'?"

"What's not an 'F'?" He looks at me like I came from Mars. "What are you talking about?"

"'F,' for ffffill-a del-fya?" I buzz my lips real loud.

He turns and knocks his forehead against mine. I smell Winstons on his breath. His eyes are really blue.

"Because it's spelled with a 'P,' that's why, you dipshit."

"Oh." I start to laugh, and his blue eyes start to crinkle at the corners, then suddenly stop. He doesn't smile. He smacks my head with his hand and messes up my hair as he gets up and runs upstairs three steps at a time.

Scottie comes back with five blue books. They aren't really books, more like heavy cardboard folders folded in three pages. Deep circles are cut into the cardboard and different dates are stamped under each one. We find a coin that matches the date and press the coin into the opening.

He rummages through the coins, sliding them all over the table. I do too.

"This is fun!" I say.

"Ah-ha! Here it is."

"What's that?"

Scottie shows me a penny.

"Eew, that's ugly," I say. I take the coin and see it has Abe Lincoln on the front and the same grassy things on the back like a regular penny, but it's dark gray. "1943, D."

"It's made out of lead." Scottie says. "During the war they didn't have any copper, so they made pennies out of lead that year, 1943."

I finger the odd penny. "How come they didn't have any copper?" I ask.

"They needed it to make guns, bullets, and stuff."

"Oh," I say. I don't know what he is talking about. How can they make pennies into guns? "That was a long time ago, I guess."

"Yeah."

"I'm lookin' for a nickel with a buffalo that has three legs," Scottie says. "A 1937, D. It's worth a lot of money." He snatches up all the nickels on the table. "When I find it, I'm gonna be rich!"

We look at money that day, and the next, and the next. I am hooked. Hooked on coins and dates and mint marks and filling up the circles in those blue books. I really like being with Scottie, too.

*   *   *

For the next few years, Scottie and I check any change we have. Pennies, dimes, nickels, and quarters give us a bond like the one between the Lone Ranger and Tonto. Scottie seems to smile at me more. He still calls me "dipshit."

*   *   *

My cool neighbor on Arbor Road lives two doors from my house. Fran likes me. Every so often I go over her house and say hello. Al, her husband, sits in his wheelchair in their living room.

"Hello, Debby," I hear Fran say even before she opens the door.

I press my face and hands against the thin glass pane and see her wave. I shout, "Hi!"

She opens the door wide.

"Hello!" Al says when I bounce into the living room. He smiles and waves "Hi" with his good hand. "It's good to have you here! You're the only little girl who visits us, you know." I give him a hug.

"It's a good thing you've come over. There is someone in the hallway that has been missing you. He's real hungry too!" Fran says. Her eyes bunch up at the corners when she smiles.

I clap my hands and smile, "I know who it is!"

Fran laughs. I tag along behind her as she goes to the hutch in the dining room. She opens the drawer and scoops up a big, handful of pennies. I follow her into the hallway.

In their hallway is a large dark cedar chest. The only thing on top of the chest is an enormous black ceramic pig: a bank. I lean my belly on the chest to reach over and pet the pig.

"Hello, Piggy," I say as I run my hand along his side. His coat is dull, but real smooth. He has a pale pink nose and a little fleck of white in each dark brown eye. Fran gives me one penny at a time. I reach further to find the slot on his back and drop in each penny. Clink, clink, clink, I love that sound. I think he was very hungry.

"It's a good thing you came over. We don't want Piggy to starve," Fran says.

"Nope," I say, as I give him one last pat on the nose. I head to the door, turn around and say, "Bye, Piggy, see you tomorrow! Bye Fran, bye Al!"

*   *   *

I sit on the stool next to the highboy and open the thin blue coin book. I see the Indian heads of twenty or so nickels. I read the date clearly on the oldest nickel, 1919. I pop the nickel out of its ninety-year-old cocoon, turn it over, and see the stately buffalo. I run my finger over its raised image, the staple animal of the Native American and pioneer alike.

One summer, my husband, Bill, and I drove through Missouri to visit our son, Gavin, in Oklahoma. We went to Tall Grass Prairie State Park. We saw herds of buffalo. We drove our car on the desolate road through the prairie. We stopped on the road while buffalo moseyed across it. At times they just stopped in the middle of the dirt road and stared at us. We were alone on the vast prairie with only buffalo and the wide-open sky. The only noise was the tread of hooves, the whicker of bison, and the wind rustling through the long grass. These animals, not often seen, transfixed us. We thought of bygone heroes who first journeyed through this barren land. We stayed there for hours, until the sun went down. No wonder this animal was chosen for the nickel; its massive size and free roaming spirit celebrated the American people.

For miles along a Missouri highway, The Biggest Gift Shop in America was advertised on billboards. We stopped at the big converted barn. It was more an antique shop or nostalgic America store. Each part of the barn was divided into eras of America, the 1920s, the 1930s, and so on. I looked for a coin bank. I yearned to find an enormous, dull, black, smooth ceramic pig with a pale pink nose and a little white fleck in each brown eye. I never found one.

*   *   *

Under his bed, my dad keeps a green metal tackle box. It has a small gold lock on it. Each year, early in November, he drags the tackle box out and hefts it on to the bed. He takes a tiny silver key from the top drawer of his dresser, puts it in the gold lock, and opens the box.

Pennies fill the bottom of the tackle box. The hinged tray that swings above the pennies is filled with silver coins. Each section of the long, narrow tray is filled with neat rows of quarters, nickels, and dimes.

I don't know when he put these coins in this box. I never saw him do it. But our whole family knows what is in that box under that bed.

I am eight years old. Dad and I spread out the coins from the tackle box on the white chenille bedspread on my parent's bed. We put them into dollar piles for the nickels, dimes, and quarters, and piles of fifty for the pennies. We count and count some more.

" . . . forty-seven, forty-eight, forty-nine, fifty," I say. I add the small pile of pennies to the already long row of penny-piles across the spread. I look closely at the penny on the top of that pile, "Hey, this is a 1936 penny, made in Philadelphia," I say.

"That's the year your mother and I were married, in Philly, too," Dad says. He stops counting, adds three piles to the line of quarters, and looks out the window. "Our anniversary is coming up. We were married on November 26, Thanksgiving Day, that year. It was the only day I had off from work."

"Keep that 1936 and put it in Scott's book," he says; he smiles and winks.

"Ok! He'll like that!" I say.

"Take another copper to replace the one you took from the pile," Dad says. "Then hurry up, or we'll never get done." Dad laughs. I laugh and wiggle on the bed, piles sliding into each other.

"You better count them again," Dad warns as he shakes his head.

"AAHH, do I *have* to?" I say, already knowing the answer. I start counting the mixed-up piles again and put them in rows. Still, every once in a while, Dad chucks me a Mercury dime or buffalo nickel that I can keep.

"Thanks!" I say, but I don't dare stop counting; it's too hard to count them over.

Dad puts all the quarters into a brown lunch bag and writes the amount on the bag in thick black pencil.

"Eighty-seven dollars and seventy-five cents," Dad says as he traces over the big numbers on the bag until they're real black.

Then, Dad's huge hand swipes the nickels off the spread and shoves them into another lunch bag. I see his lips moving, he's counting. He does the same with the dimes. He writes the total on the bags.

Dad puts all the pennies in a big brown paper grocery bag. When all the coins are put in bags, Dad lines them across the bed and adds the numbers up on a piece of paper.

After a while, Dad stands up and says, "$169.82." He circles the total on the paper four times.

"Thanks for your help!" He smiles at me. He closes the empty tackle box, slides the lock on, and clicks it shut. Then, he shoves the tackle box back under the bed and drops the key in the top drawer of his dresser.

I go find Scottie to show him the coins Dad gave me.

Dad gets in the station wagon and goes to the bank. He cashes in the coins at the PSFS—the Philadelphia Savings Fund Society—bank at the corner of Front Street and Cheltenham Avenue. When he comes home, he gives the money to my mother for our Thanksgiving dinner. Whatever is left over is her money for Christmas presents.

*   *   *

My brother Kennie is a year older than me; he's ten. He's skinny, has light brown hair and blue eyes. Though I want to be his friend, he never wants to play with me. But today, he does.

Kennie and I roll a pink rubber ball across the floor of the living room at our house on Arbor Road. I sit against the sofa, and he is across the room by the stairs. We spread our legs out wide and roll the ball real fast to each other. If it goes outside our legs the person who rolled it gets a letter. If you spell P-I-G, you lose. After each of us has a turn, we close our legs a little bit and roll the ball again.

I'm winning. Kennie fires the ball at me. It hits my knee, bounces off the coffee table to the right, and rolls under the sofa.

"You dork!" I snap. I sprawl on my belly and shove my hand under the flap of the sofa.

"Where'd it go?" I stick my face under the flap into total darkness. Then, I see the ball at the back of the sofa near the wall. I can't reach it. I get up and squeeze sideways behind the sofa. I suck in my tummy to fit.

"Hurry up!" Kennie says.

"You shouldn't've rolled it so fast!" I say as I kick the ball. It flies out the front of the sofa. Kennie runs after it.

Then, near my foot I see a nickel next to the wall. I reach down to pick it up; my head gets stuck on top of the sofa, but my hand searches for it. I find it and grab it. I turn my face to the wall and shove the nickel in my mouth, so Kennie won't see what I found.

"Come on, let's play!" Kennie says.

We play some more. I laugh when the game ends, because Kennie's got P-I-G. He's doesn't think it's funny.

"Shut up, dork," he says.

Then, we watch *The Three Stoogies* on TV.

I laugh out loud at Curly. He's so funny. "Ha-haaaa-ug!" I gulp. The nickel slides quickly down my throat.

"Mommy!!" I clutch my neck and run to the kitchen. "I swallowed a nickel!"

Mommy rushes from the stove to me and whacks me on the back real hard. I gulp for air and think my eyes will pop out of my head. She whacks me hard again.

"Mommy, stop! It hurts!" I yell.

"Where does your throat hurt?" Mommy asks. She spins me around, jams her hand in my mouth, pries my mouth open like a can of tuna fish, and searches down my throat for the nickel. I gasp for air again.

I yank her hand out of my mouth. "Mommy, my throat doesn't hurt! My back does!" "Oh." Mom's frightened eyes look at my face. She holds me tight and rubs my back. Her eyes are red.

My brother Scottie comes in the back door and slams it shut so hard the rooster picture on the wall swings like the doohickie on the cuckoo clock in the living room.

"What's for dinner?" he says, then adds, "What's the matter?" He looks at Mommy, then me.

"Debby swallowed a nickel," Mommy says.

"Oh," he says and throws his jacket on the chair. "Whaddaya do that for?" He lifts the lid of the pot on the stove. "Did it have a buffalo on it?"

"I dunno," I say. I look at my feet. "I forgot to look."

"You dipshit."

"Ahhhh, why do you always yell at me!" I cry out. I feel my face get hot and my eyes get watery.

"Scott, don't call her that. Why do you do that to your sister?" I hide my face in Mom's red apron and cry. "You should love your sister and not be so mean!!"

"Sorry, Mom. Yeah, I . . . do," he spits out. He turns and stirs the pot.

Mommy rubs her eyes with the back of her hand, then wipes my face with her apron. She hugs me real tight, then says, "Well, I guess we'll see that nickel again in a few days."

Startled, I look up at her face. "Whaddaya mean, Mommy?"

Scottie starts to laugh as he takes a big slice of roast beef out of the pot on the stove, dunks it in the gravy, and sticks the whole thing in his wide-open mouth. He heads out of the kitchen in stitches. "It meanshh it'll come out in your schhhhittt!"

"Scott Randall! You stop that right now!!" Mom hollers. She covers my ears with her hands.

"Mommm-mieee! Ahhhhh," I scream. I don't understand it all, but it doesn't sound good.

Scottie is still laughing out loud as he walks to the living room. I cry even harder when I hear him say, "Guess what the goofy, dipshit did?" Kennie's hoots of laughter set Scottie off laughing even louder.

"Scott Randall!! Kenneth Richard!!" Mom shouts as she holds my ears with her rough hands. "Stop that!"

I look up. Is Mommy crying? I look closer; no, no tears. I hug her tight; she cradles my head in her arms.

"Mommy, I love you."

The nickel I swallowed was not a buffalo nickel.
That's all I'm going to say about that.

*   *   *

When I was a kid, money, to me, was coins. I was paid fifty cents allowance. I shined my father's and brother's work shoes for a quarter a pair. I never had any paper money;

besides, coins were much better. I put my money in a green plastic dinosaur, a promotional gift from the local Sinclair gas station. I liked the weight of it and the sound of change rattling around inside it. Paper money didn't make any noise.

*　　*　　*

It's 1964 and Scottie is moving to Florida. He packs up "the red roach," his ugly maroon Chevy. Before he leaves, though, he gives me his coin collection, the five blue cardboard books with the coins we had looked for, and found, over all those years. I am happy about the collection, but not sure what it means to move to Florida. I worry that I might not see him again.

I shouldn't have worried. Scottie was back in a week. Something or other hadn't worked out.

"Hey, dipshit, can I have my coin books back?" Scottie said at dinner one night.

Blue eyes met blue eyes.

"No," I said as I sipped my milk.

Mom laughed out loud. "Good for you, Debby! Scott if you give someone something, it's for keeps," she said. "Don't be an Indian giver . . . and don't call her that name!"

*　　*　　*

I am thankful Scottie gave me a love of coins. I realize, too, that I wouldn't have that love of coins if I ran away when Scottie yelled at me in the dining room that long ago afternoon. Those quarters, nickels, dimes, and pennies gave Scottie and me a bond we'd never had before. Even though his interests went from coins to cars, to fishing, to sailboats, I always liked change. As time went by, I realized that saving change, like Dad did, came in handy.

*   *   *

On August 29, 1972, Bill and I get engaged. I am eighteen. I worked in the Political Science Department at Temple University in Philadelphia as a secretary until we got married, on March 24, 1973.

Every Friday is payday at Temple. I walk down Broad Street to the Fidelity Bank near the corner of Columbia Avenue to deposit my check.

"May I please have ten nickels, ten dimes and ten quarters?" I ask the teller when I hand her my check and deposit ticket. "Can I have a roll of quarters, too?" I add.

"Umm-huh," the teller mumbles. She barely looks up from her adding machine as she punches in my check amount and deducts the coin total. She turns, spreads a bunch of coins on the counter, and zings them into an envelope. With a lavish swoop of her hand, she pulls down the lever on the right side of the adding machine and then rips off the paper stub at the top.

"$56.34, inta yer a'count," the teller mumbles. She grabs a roll of quarters wrapped in faded orange paper and slaps it on top of the envelope and paper stub and shoves them across the counter, never once looking up from her work. "Obliged," she barks.

She shoos me away and advances the next person in line, all with one jerk of her wrist. Then, she barks, "Next!" when the man behind me doesn't move up to the counter fast enough.

I scoot outside the bank and walk up Broad Street. Amid the noise of cars and buses, I hear the jingle of the coins in my purse. *Clink, clink, clink!* I love that sound. It reminds me of when I was a kid.

I get to my office and dump the coins out on my desk. I count out a quarter, nickel, dime: forty cents. I make ten piles of forty cents. Two piles, eighty cents, go each into five crumpled envelopes, labeled Monday through Friday. I fold each of them carefully into a little square. I tuck my bus fare for next week into my purse.

When I get home from work, I break open the faded orange paper on the roll of quarters and put them in the large whiskey bottle Scottie gave to me. I put ten dollars in quarters in it every week.

*　　*　　*

On December 8, 1972, I cash in the whiskey bottle of quarters. My mother and I go to Frieda's Bridal Salon on Torresdale Avenue in Philadelphia, and I buy my wedding dress with my savings. It is a gorgeous white dress, with a nine-foot train. A matching head piece with a twelve-foot veil comes with it. It costs me my entire "quarter" savings, $125, but I love it. I am on cloud nine!

*　　*　　*

Bill and I have five children, two sons and three daughters. We are a happy, healthy family, but we don't have a lot of money. We have put our trust in God a lot, for our family and for what little money we have. I manage Bill's once-a-month paycheck, but the last two weeks of the month are always a nightmare. Someone always needs shoes or clothes; we eat a lot of hot dogs and homemade soup. The whiskey bottle is useless. It's in the back of the closet in my bedroom. It has only a few pennies in it, some buttons, a bunch of Light-Bright pegs, and a yellow crayon.

However, on my kitchen counter I do keep a tall ceramic bank that looks like an ice cream sundae. It never has many coins in it, either.

"Mom, can I buy lunch today? It's pizza!" Wendy says.

"Yeah, Mom, me too!" Greg says.

Even though the children are on the reduced lunch program, and they only buy lunch once a week, the forty cents for lunch is still a struggle. I tip over the ice cream bank. The pitted rubber stopper with its worn edges pops out easily. I dump out what money there is and count: "Quarter, nickel, dime—there's one lunch; quarter, nickel. . . one, two, three, four, five, six—" I grab my purse and root for more money. I find four pennies! "— yes!" I swish the money off the counter into my hand and put it in two beat-up envelopes.

"Mom, can I have pizza too?" Gavin whispers as he tugs on my sweater.

I look at the big blue eyes of my little tow-headed first grader. "Let me see," I say.

I scour my purse again and find a dime. I hurry to the closet, rummage through the pocket of my jacket, then the pocket of Bill's raincoat. I find two nickels and a quarter. **"Thank you, Lord!"** The quarter, dime, and one nickel go into Gavin's envelope. I put it in his red book bag. The kids wave to me as they ride to school with my friend Carol and her kids.

"There, we made it through another 'school lunch' day with a nickel to spare," I say to three-year-old Abbey.

I've been reading the Bible more lately. It says we should be good stewards of our money. I'm not quite sure what that means, or how to do it, especially when I never have much money.

I see baby Cami is asleep in her swing. I scoop Abbey up in my arms and go into the kitchen. I sit her on the counter and let her put the extra nickel in the slot of the empty ice cream sundae bank. She laughs when it makes a dull clunk on the bottom of the bank. I smile but turn as I help her down. I don't like that hollow sound.

*   *   *

Now, in the twenty-first century, most kids won't pick up a coin from the floor. Yesterday at the local high school where I work, I found a penny in the hall. I picked one up with the same rush of excitement that I got when I fished to the bottom of the cereal box to find the prize. Maybe kids today think that penny is worthless. Maybe they won't stoop low to pick something off the ground. There's an old saying, "Don't stop the parade for a penny." I would stop and pick up that penny and mess up the parade to boot.

*   *   *

As an assistant in the Life Skills class for special education students at the local high school, I gave each of the students a small ceramic piggy bank. They had to sign an agreement that they would save money and not take any money out of it. The paper had to be signed by a parent too. The motto for the piggy bank challenge was, "If you don't take care of a penny, you'll never take care of a dollar."

In June, after eight months, they each brought in their bank, and we counted all their money. They were all surprised how much was in their banks. J.T. won ten dollars for first place. He had $35.73. He said he had to keep the pig in his locker at school because his dad steals his money.

The kids had fun with this assignment. I hope they learned a lesson from it. God used J.T. to teach me a good lesson too: you never know where these kids are coming from.

Maybe these students will keep their banks for a long time to come. Maybe they will remember the teacher who gave them a bank. Maybe they will pay it forward and give someone else a bank.

*   *   *

Our children gave Bill and me a trip to London for Mother's and Father's Day and my graduating from college in 2005. At the gift shop at Westminster Abbey, I bought a bank: a red, metal London phone booth. It has glass-paned sides and a rounded top, just like those charming red phone booths in London. It sits on my kitchen counter, the coins visible from across the room. It's my favorite bank. It reminds me of the best vacation ever, from the best kids in the world.

*One of my favorite Bible stories is the one of the widow's mites—in our day, two mites would equal one penny. The woman had only two small coins, or mites, and gave them as her offering. Others gave only a portion of their wealth, but **she gave all** she had. The red phone booth reminds me of that story, perhaps because I bought it at Westminster Abbey. It also reminds me that*

God cares about even the smallest things, like two mites, or the assistant who gave piggy banks to special kids.

*   *   *

One recent Christmas I wrapped up twenty-seven big, white piggy banks for my sons, daughters, nieces, nephews, brothers, sisters, family friends, teachers, and neighbors. Every one of them was excited and most of them said they have never had an actual pig for a bank.

Any time one of our children brought a friend home from college to stay the weekend, I gave them a bank. Sometimes I gave banks that were sailboats, bunnies, cows, or cars, but most of the time they were just pigs. I hope they will be good stewards, caretakers, of the money they have.

Colleagues at school, newlyweds, graduates, and new babies also get a bank. Most people tell me they keep their loose change in a jar, a coffee can, or some kind of a dish, usually on their dresser or by their sink. Now they have someplace special to put their change.

Occasionally, I will get a letter and someone will say, "Do you remember the bank you gave me?" Then, they'll tell me how surprised they were at how much money was in it and what they bought with it. These banks have become gossamer strands that keep us together.

*   *   *

I still save coins. I have a big white bunny with brown eyes. She sits on the bookcase in our den. There is a big black bear and large purple pig in the den too. But I'll never forget what it's like to have no money: to search through jackets or slide my hand down the seat of the sofa to find money for lunch or bus fare, or to tip over a coin bank and hear nothing rattle inside.

*So, when I cash my coins in now, I give that money away, anonymously, to someone who can use a bit of help. That bunny, bear, and pig have helped pay someone's rent, buy groceries, purchase new appliances when old ones broke, and pay for car repairs. The Lord has shown me the joy of giving. But I believe I had to witness what it was like to be in need, for myself, to know the joy of giving. I do not want any thanks. I have learned that the joy of being able to give is the greatest feeling in the world. The Lord is right: it **is** more blessed to give than to receive.*

*   *   *

Scottie retired a few years ago after forty years as an electrician. He and his wife, Dot, live in Ohio near their children and grandchildren.

Scottie laughs when I call and tell him I found the old blue coin books. I open the folder and look at the nickels again as I talk to him.

"Did you ever find that three-legged buffalo nickel?" I ask.

"No, but I still look for it. Everybody wants one of them," he says. I hear him take a draw from his cigarette. He laughs and says, "Yup, I'm gonna be rich when I find it!"

We laugh and talk about the weather, our kids, and old times.

"Well, Scottie, it was good to talk to you. I have to go. I love you."

"I love you, too, Debby. Good-bye." he says.

*   *   *

I open the top drawer of the old highboy and slide the thin blue book of old nickels on top of the four other blue books that have worn cardboard edges and a bit of mildew.

Suddenly, I turn, and laugh out loud.

I just realized: Scottie doesn't call me "dipshit" anymore.

Mother and Marilyn

When I was growing up and happy collecting change with Scottie, another type of change was happening in our family—a change I knew little about. Life was not happy during that time, for the rest of my family.

As I got older, I tried to understand it better, but the only events I envisioned were through the mist of the seldom-mentioned past.

Two years before I was born, my sister, Marilyn, died. They say she died of childhood diabetes. Marilyn was sick on June 29 and 30 and she died on July 1, 1951. She was buried on my mom's birthday at Greenmount Cemetery, in Philadelphia. My maternal grandmother, Ernestina Godwin, gave my parents her gravesite plot because my parents couldn't afford one. Marilyn was buried in the same plot as my grandfather, my mother's father, John Godwin—yes, a double-decker grave.

My brother Frankie was thirteen at the time; Ronnie was eleven, and Scottie was nine. To me, that explains why Scottie picked on me. Maybe he didn't want to get close to another sister. It hurt too much to lose someone you loved. Maybe he even wished I was Marilyn.

Now I realize that the look on Mom's face when I swallowed the nickel was terror. She was scared to death that she would lose another child. Scottie laughing and calling me names, even though he was a teenager, I think, hurt her deeply.

Growing up, Marilyn's name was never mentioned in our house. Mom only ever talked to me about Marilyn a handful of times in my life.

I know Mom carried the burden of Marilyn's death a long time. However, after Mom died in 2006, at age ninety-one, I found a letter from her inside a box of three dolls she had kept that were Marilyn's. She wanted someone who knew Marilyn to take care of the dolls. Mother wrote: "I have carried this burden of her death for long enough. I am laying it along the side of the road and going on." The letter was dated, December 1979.

I gave the dolls and the letter to my brother Ronnie.

Humble Pie, Yum

God was speaking to me,
  But I didn't listen.
He let me go on with my stubborn ways,
  And I floundered.
I begged Him to straighten out everyone else.
  But, with His patient, gentle hand,
    He straightened *me* out instead.

It's late autumn of 1990. Wendy is sixteen and a junior in high school. She is a straight "A" student in high school, and she plays flute and piccolo in the high school band and orchestra.

For the past year she has been active in a local church, a different one than I go to, and actively attends their youth group. Wendy is happy and anxious to go to church, for which I am thrilled. She goes on Sundays and to youth group on Sunday and Wednesday nights. She has a glow about her. It must be the Lord working in her. But she also has some nutty ideas.

After dinner, the kitchen is its usual mess. Some of the dirty plates are strewn across the counter with silverware angled across them like the hands of a sick clock. The rest of the plates are still on the dining room table with the rice hardening in sticky ham gravy.

Well, we got through another dinner. There was enough ham and the kids always like the rice. Maybe tomorrow I'll make some soup with the small ham bone. The kids hate "ham soup." It's really bean soup, but if I called it that, they would really, really hate it. I think there are a couple of green peppers, and a few onions left out in the garden. They are essential in ham soup.

Bill is in the garden now, taking the tomato stakes out of the ground. I look out the window and see he has some green tomatoes in a basket and two red ones on top. Lined up on the edge of the garden wall are six green peppers and two small onions. Good, they'll be dinner tomorrow night. Maybe I'll make popovers too. The kids love them.

I hear Greg upstairs practicing his saxophone. Bill's Uncle Lou would be proud, since he gave Greg his old sax. Gavin is typing his term paper on the word processor in the tiny back room. Abbey and Cami bring out the salt and pepper, butter, mustard, and ketchup from the dining room and put them away. My hands are in the dishpan again; the water is really hot and soapy. I wash a few serving bowls, rinse them, and put them in the drainer. Wendy comes in the kitchen with another stack of dirty plates.

"Ugh, Wendy, you shouldn't stack the plates together because then I have to rinse off both sides of them," I say.

"Mom, we have a dishwasher," she says.

"Yeah, I know, but I don't run it after dinner every night. I only run it when it's full, and stuff gets stuck on the plates when they sit."

"Does it matter?" she asks. Not waiting for an answer, she disappears back into the dining room.

"It does to me," I say to no one. I rinse the food off the fronts and backs of four more plates.

Wendy brings in some glasses, empties a few in the sink, then puts all of them in the top rack of the dishwasher. Abbey and Cami throw the napkins from the table in the trash and head out of the kitchen.

"Make sure you do your homework before the TV goes on," I call to them.

The girls don't answer. I hear the back door open, then shut, and I see them run to Bill in the garden.

I scrape the baked-on ham off the bottom of the pan, rinse it into the garbage disposal, then push the pan under the hot dishwater. I use a scrubbie and some real muscle to clean the pan. Gunky water splashes, dotting my white shirt with brown wet spots.

"Oh, phooey," I say. I wipe the hair off my face with the back of my hand.

The pan is steamy when I lift it out of the water and I see the corners are still crusty, so I dunk it again and scrub the corners, then rinse it. I make more spots on my shirt. Now the pan is clean, and my shirt's a real mess.

But it's my hands I look at most: they're red and sore looking. The pan clatters when I drop it in the dish drainer, and I dry my hands on a dish towel. My hands don't look any better when they're dry. My wide gold wedding band is wedged between swollen creases of red skin on my finger. The other fingers are red and wrinkled. I look away, remembering hands exactly like these, same wide band and all: the hands of Mrs. Miller, my Sunday School teacher at Berachah Church in Cheltenham when I was about twelve. It's funny what triggers memories. I haven't thought of her in years.

I liked Mrs. Miller and her lessons a lot. She was fun to be with; her dark brown hair was thick and straight, and her brown eyes sparkled. She was short and not quite fat, but almost. We would sit on metal folding chairs in a small circle, the five girls in the junior high class, and she would read Bible stories to us, then put them into modern-day perspective. I remember she told us the story of Martha and Mary. Wow, how'd I remember that, too? And then she would pray. She had the softest, most beautiful, sincere voice.

I look at the clock, 7:45. I really don't have time to think about Mrs. Miller. I must straighten up the dining room and kitchen and fold laundry. Then I must look at the check book. Ugh. I always have to finagle money, sapping what little savings we have to get through to the end of the month. I take the dish cloth and wipe the counter.

"Mom," Wendy says from behind me, breaking me out of my daze.

"Yeah," I say. I don't turn around, as I'm taking the burners off the gas stove and cleaning under them. Wendy comes closer.

"Can I go to Japan?"

I turn and stare. "Are you kidding me?" I smile, laugh, and shake my head from side to side. She must be delirious; maybe she ate too much rice tonight.

"No, I'm not kidding," she says. "The youth group is going on a mission trip and I want to go. They leave in

June, for five weeks. It's only seven months away! And I'm already taking Japanese at school, so Mom, please? It's only nine hundred dollars." She stands up straight. I can sense her determination.

"Nine hundred dollars!" I home in on the money issue as I shake my head and smirk. "We can just about afford to keep this family going with this new house, and you kids. Where do you think I'd get the money to send you there? *And* do you actually think I would let my sixteen-year-old daughter fly halfway across the globe?" I look up to the ceiling, take a deep breath, bite my lips, and turn my head.

Lord, do I need this added to my plate now? My quiver is full, my plate is full, and I don't know how to handle what I have, no less this child with a goofy idea.

"Come on, Mom. Teresa is going," Wendy says. "She has a plan for me to fund my trip."

"You gonna go beg people for money?" I ask. I see her flinch at my words. "I don't think so! Not my daughter!" I throw the dish rag in the sink and turn towards the window and look outside. I see Bill pick up the basket of tomatoes and the peppers. The girls swing on the swings.

"It's called fundraising, Mom," Wendy says, her green eyes filling with unshed tears. "Come on, Mom, pretty please?"

Teresa is one of the youth leaders at church who's befriended Wendy. I don't like this idea she's planting in her head of begging for money. Plus, that gallivanting across the world idea, well that just takes the cake! Why is it kids think they are wiser than their parents? How come they listen to people they hardly know and fall for whatever they say? I turn around to Wendy and plant my feet hard into the shabby kitchen throw rug.

I look her straight in the eye.

'No. Absolutely not. That's my answer," I say as I straighten my back and cross my arms. She looks away.

"What's your answer?" Bill asks as he comes in the kitchen and plops the vegetable basket on the counter. Dirt falls through the wicker onto the green Formica counter.

"My answer is *final*, that's what it is." I take a deep breath and shake my head. I exhale in disgust and walk out of the room, throwing my arms up in the air.

"Oh," Bill looks wide-eyed from me to Wendy. "What's final?"

I don't hang around to talk about it anymore. I grab a basket of clean laundry and head upstairs. When I reach the foot of the stairs, I hear her say, "Dad, Mom just doesn't understand ..."

I go up to our room, close the door, drop the basket of clothes on the old red shag carpet, and flop across the bed. *Lord, where does she come up with these friends and crazy ideas? Nine hundred dollars! I don't know how we're going to make it to the end of the month, and she wants to go where? Halfway around the world? If the world is twenty-four thousand miles around, she'll be twelve thousand miles away. Oy vey! Lord, You gotta knock some sense into her little head. What's she thinking? No, she's not thinking at all, that's it, she's not thinking at all. This will pass, I know it will. Lord, You will have to straighten this mess out. Thank you, Lord.*

I reach for my Bible on the nightstand. I see my hands again. The knuckles are sore. I look closely and see that the tips of my thumbs and two knuckles are starting to crack. I spread lotion on them again and then again.

Lord, I diapered that girl when she was a baby with these hands, I held her with these hands, fed her with these hands. These hands have worked for her, and for You, Lord. I've taken care of this little lamb You gave us. Wendy is the friend I prayed for before she was born, and You answered my prayer. Now Lord, You take care of her. Yes, help me believe and know that You are in control here.

I reach for my Bible and turn to the story of Martha and Mary. I picture Mrs. Miller's rough hands flipping through the pages of her worn Bible, to this exact story. My hands look identical. Here it is, in the book of Luke. "Jesus and his disciples came to the house of a woman named Martha for dinner." I read on, "And she had a sister called Mary, who sat at Jesus' feet and heard His word. But Martha was distracted with much serving, and she approached Him and said, 'Lord, do You not care that my sister has left me to serve alone? Therefore, tell her to help me.' And Jesus answered and said to her. 'Martha, Martha, you are worried and troubled about many things. But one thing is needed, and Mary has chosen that good part, which will not be taken away from her.'"

I shut my Bible and shove it across the bed. "Humph," I say.

The subject of Japan does not pass. It just gets buried for a while, a good long while. I pray each day that God will answer my prayers and give me wisdom as a parent. I know He answers prayers, I have confidence in Him. I have for a lot of years.

Japan is not mentioned again, not by Wendy or by me. Life is normal. Our finances are real tight, though. I really must look for some kind of work. The last time I had a job was before Cami was born. I worked at Burger King, from 5 p.m. to 1 a.m. The hardest part was wondering if Bill was going to be home in time for me to get to work on time. He didn't think he should leave his job so I could work. But he did.

I worked there for six months. My mother would say to me, "Debby, you're spreading yourself too thin. You can't work at home during the day, then go to work for eight hours at night! Forget about the darn money! Enjoy being with those kids while they're young. God knows what you need. He'll take care of you! Let Bill go get another job. That family business doesn't pay him enough anyway."

Mother was right; I knew that. But I bristled when *she* said it. Bill has never questioned his pay. He just accepts what he is given. I must honor and respect him for that choice. That is the type of man he is.

However, I am the one who pays the bills—the bills that are mounting up. I think of Martha more and more. I feel her frustration, her aloneness. I can't cut back anymore. I even re-roast the coffee grounds I use each morning. I dump them in a pie plate and put them in the lower oven, where the pilot light is, and they dry out perfectly for the next day's morning pot.

I did apply to work at the local bank and grocery store. I passed their entrance tests, but was told that they have revolving schedules, and I would have to work different hours and different days every week. I can't do that. I must work at night and have regular hours. I spend several more days applying at WaWa, the local convenience store, and several offices. I'm getting down. I feel like no one wants me, like I'm beating my head against a wall.

One spring evening while sitting in the den, Wendy says to me, "Mom, I still want to go to Japan."

"Really?" I sigh and say, "I've been praying that problem would go away," but I smile at her. She laughs at me. I turn toward her and shift my legs under me on the threadbare yellow sofa. She smiles back. I can talk about this now, sorta. *Lord, I will be like Mary, and I will listen, really listen.* I chew on my lip.

"Mom, I've been fundraising and I already have $415."

"And how did you do that?" I ask. I see her green eyes twinkle.

She hands me a folded yellow piece of paper with a full-page letter on it. I read it through and am immediately drawn to the complete dedication to the work that the mission team will do in Japan. I stop myself short, though, not to be coerced. I fold the letter and give it back to her.

"Mom, I sent it to people I know: aunts, uncles, teachers, neighbors."

She sees my surprise.

"Mom, people want to support me. They want to help! If you let me go, the money I raise will go towards my trip. If not, then they'll split the money with other kids who are going."

"My answer is still no," I say. She looks at me for what seems to be a long time, says nothing, gets up and walks away.

*   *   *

A few days later, the telephone rings. It's my dear friend Eleanor, from our former church. We don't talk very often nowadays, but she'll always be my good friend. I can hear the urgency in her voice.

"Debby, please pray for my daughter. I don't know where she is!"

"What's the matter, Eleanor? Is she with anybody? What's going on?" I fire all these questions at her in a matter of seconds. Her daughter, Holly, is the same age as Wendy; they used to go to Sunday school together.

She tells me Holly got in with the wrong crowd at school. She's pregnant and has been withdrawn and strange lately. She's missed school a lot. She left home this morning and hasn't come back. It's now ten at night.

"I'll pray right away for her, Eleanor. God knows where she is, and He'll take care of her wherever she goes."

"Oh, thank you. Yes, please pray for her, and for me too." I can feel the desperation in her voice.

"I will, most definitely. Eleanor, please call me when she comes home. She'll be home soon. Don't worry. I love you. Good-bye."

I hang up the phone on the wall and pray right away for both. I'm surprised to hear of their trouble. I didn't know Eleanor had a daughter with such problems! I flop down on the big chair in the den and say it again, this time out loud, "I didn't know Holly had such problems!"

I bolt upright and think about what I just said. *Holly has a problem.*

It's like God jerked my arm and said to me, "Yes, Holly has a problem. But Wendy has an *opportunity!*"

Wendy has an opportunity, a great opportunity to go to Japan. **Why did I not see that before?** She gets to go with a church group of fifteen kids and seven leaders. They have houses to stay in, food to eat, and most of all work to do—work God wants them to do!

I get up and run upstairs and knock on Wendy's bedroom door.

"Come in."

I stroll in, smile, and sit on the edge of her bed. I smile some more. I'm just about ready to burst!

She looks at me and turns her head slightly, closes her eyes a bit, as if to say, what's going on? But she remains silent.

I smile and show my teeth, my eyes become little slits because my cheeks are so fat and puffed out with my smile.

"Mom, what's up? What are you giving me that goofy smile for?" She laughs, then stops short. She raises her eyebrows and flaps her arms out to the side, palms up.

"What?" she yells.

"Wendy, you have my blessing to go to Japan," I say.

"Really!! Are you sure?" She jumps up off her bed, tripping over the biology and calculus books on the floor.

"Yes, I am sure! Go and do the work God wants you to do, and . . ."

I don't get to finish my sentence because she throws her arms around my neck and yells, "I knew I would go! I knew God would answer our prayers! I guess Dad was praying too! What changed your mind?"

"God works in strange ways; that's all I'll say." She hugs me tight, and I laugh into her long brown hair.

So, maybe Wendy and Bill were in cahoots all along. I smile, close my eyes, and hug her again.

I will tell Wendy about the phone call I just had a bit later. But for now, I love the look on her face, and the strength in her hug. I love the peace I feel.

*   *   *

Wendy did go to Okinawa, Japan, for five weeks in July 1991. She had a wonderful time. Their group set up summer Bible schools in different locations, held youth rallies, spread the good news of the Gospel, and she made lots of new friends with whom she corresponded for years.

Eleanor called the next day that Holly was home. She had a perfect little baby boy six months later.

The week before I told Wendy her good news, I applied to work at the local WaWa convenience store. Then, *after* I told her she could go to Japan, I got a call to interview there. But I thought to myself, "Gee, Wendy gets to go to Japan, and I get to work at WaWa." Somehow, it just didn't seem fair to me.

However, the Lord does work in strange ways. Before my interview at WaWa, a local chiropractor called and asked me if I was still interested in working in his office, at a rate of eight dollars an hour—twice as much as WaWa! I said, "Yes, I'd love to!"

Maybe the Lord made me struggle financially because of my stubbornness with Wendy's mission, or maybe because of my lack of faith? I don't know, but Wendy, like Mary, was listening to God's voice. And, just like Martha, I was only thinking about me. God grabbed my attention and made me listen to Him through a desperate phone call from a friend.

I know that my life changed for the better once I really listened to God's voice. I look down at my hands now. They are still red and rough, but I think Mrs. Miller would be proud of me.

I do wonder if Martha ever really listened, too.

Elizabeth

*T*here is something wonderful to tell about her life, even though she feels it has been most ordinary. Her name is Elizabeth Off. She is quiet and shy. She has rosy cheeks, a wry sense of humor, and more ambition than someone half her age. She loves her family, flowers, and the color pink; but most of all, she loves the Lord. Elizabeth is my mother-in-law; her son, Bill, is my husband. Yes, she is the same woman I shied away from as a young bride. I now confess my great love, honor, and admiration for her gracious life, love, and unfailing spirit.

I enter her tiny living room lit by a small lamp in the corner. Elizabeth sits on the end cushion of the sofa near the soft light. She smiles at me and says a hearty "hello," even though her voice is very soft. Mom's bright eyes are a pale green, and they twinkle when she smiles like she knows something that I don't. Her black hair defies her age; only a few strands of silver hair highlight her temples.

Mom is dressed in a navy-blue jacket embroidered with pale blue and off-white flowers along its front edge; an ecru blouse finishes the neckline. A small crimson blanket covers part of her lap. A matching navy skirt covers the tips of her knees, revealing thin legs, small feet in pale blue slippers, and one swollen, puffy ankle resting on a small pillow. She laughs when she tells me how she fell off the adult tricycle her children bought for her.

"The thing was so hard to steer, the seat slanted forward, and down I went!" she said as she slaps her hands on her lap. "I've ridden a two-wheeler for seventy years, and I'm just not used to that thing!" Her voice is the loudest it can be, yet it is still soft to my ear. Then, peering down at her sore ankle she laughs at herself and says, "I thank the Lord I didn't break anything." She smiles and adds, "I *really* do thank Him."

I sit across from her. Mom picks up a funny-looking thing from the table. She sees that I am wondering what it is. It has the handle of a screwdriver, with a long hairpin-like end.

"It's a button hook!" she says. Even though her fingers are enlarged at the knuckles and a bit bent, her small hands work quickly passing the hairpin-end through her buttonhole, hooking the button, and pulling it through.

Mom recalls her Grandmother Lerch using a button hook on her high button shoes. Her Grandfather Lerch was called "Squire." Mom believes that was the term for a mayor of a town. They owned a farm in Tinicum, Pennsylvania. Grandfather Lerch was a heavy man. When she visited the farm as a little girl, Mom would tie Grandpa's shoes for him, since he had a hard time bending over.

Mom was born in Philadelphia in 1925, the sixth child of Ida and Walter Myers. Three months before Mom was born, her father died suddenly while sitting on the front porch of their house. Her mother, Grandma, raised her children by herself and never remarried. Money was tight for everyone during the Depression, but Grandma was very, very poor. They had little to eat and few things to wear. But they had each other, and they attended a strong church and had great faith in God. They walked to the store and to their church services. The kids walked from Philadelphia, over the Ben Franklin Bridge, to the church school in Camden. Mom remembers cutting cardboard from a cereal box to put in her shoes to cover the holes in the soles.

The church school was in Camden because children who went to school in New Jersey didn't have to be vaccinated. Their faith did not believe in medical assistance; they depended on God for health and healing. Mom said Grandma instilled in them that God would always provide, and that God was good. It wasn't always easy; it wasn't always pleasant.

Mom recalls often not having enough food to eat, only crackers to nibble. Then, someone would leave a bag of groceries on their front steps or give them some potatoes. God provided. Grandma was a substitute schoolteacher who worked at the church school. Mom's oldest brother was nine years older than her. When he was twelve, he went to work at the Apex Hosiery mill a few blocks from their house. His earnings helped feed the family.

Mom remembered one bitter cold day a man came to their front door, not far from being frozen solid. He asked if he could have some food. Grandma told him to come in and they shared whatever food they had with him. He thanked them and left after dinner; they never saw the man again. I asked Mom if she thought that was strange. Her eyes held that twinkle and said she believed that man was an angel. She quoted Hebrews 13:2, "Be not forgetful to entertain strangers: for thereby some have entertained angels unawares."

Mom shifts the blanket on her lap and peeks past her knees to her swollen foot. She smiles thinking again of riding that big tricycle. She tells about her first ride on a two-wheeler.

Aunt Myrt, Mom's sister, had seven young children. When Mom was a young girl, she would help Myrt and her husband, Ozzie, with the children. They were poor too. Mom loved her nieces and nephews and helped care for them from the time they were infants. Once, Ozzie gave her a quarter for helping with the children. Mom shifts her foot on the soft pillow and giggles. She took that quarter to Pennypack Park in Philadelphia and rented a bicycle for the entire twenty-five cents! But she had never been on a bicycle in her life, so she got on and fell off, got on and fell off, got on again and fell off in a ditch! Then, she *was determined* she was going to ride that bike and get her money's worth out of that quarter. She got on the bike, started pedaling fast, and rode all around the park that whole day. Mom laughed and said she wanted to learn to ride because it looked like so much fun when she watched other people.

A turning point in Mom's life was after she left school in the tenth grade. She went to work at James G. Biddle Company in Center City, Philadelphia, on an assembly line of electrical testing instruments. She was removed from her sheltered world of family and church to where people had all kinds of boyfriends and girlfriends, used language she wasn't used to, and voiced their feelings and anger out loud. One time, Mom's boss told her to do a co-worker's job while they were on vacation. Mom was shocked when the co-worker, a woman, returned and screamed at Mom for taking over her job!

Though Mom was out in the big world, she wasn't swayed by its crudeness. She was still dedicated to the Lord. She went to work, then went home to her mother and family. She loved her church and continued to help others in any way she could.

I go over to the large bookcase and bring the portrait of Dad to Mom. She takes the picture lovingly in her hands, and says it was taken a few weeks before their wedding. He was so handsome. Her voice trails away as she recalls the love they shared.

Mom was twenty-two years old. Her brothers and sisters were all married; she and Grandma lived together. One August day in 1947, a widower from church, George Off, came to call at their home. He stayed and talked to Grandma and Mom. He was forty-two, and a fine gentleman. They had known each other in church for many years.

George lived in New Jersey near the coast, with his five children, ages seven to twenty-one. He was raised in Merion, Pennsylvania. His father was a wealthy stockbroker who also owned the Brighton Hotel on the Atlantic City boardwalk. George's mother's family owned Allens Department Store, an upscale store in the Germantown section of Philadelphia. George moved to the shore and worked in the hotel with his father, but he hated it. He wanted to be growing plants and working with his hands.

George left the hotel business, built some greenhouses, and opened a flower shop. He grew flowers, specializing in orchids, and made floral arrangements for his father's hotel. He also sold flowers in his retail store. However, after his first wife passed away, George gave the business to his brother, Lou, with the stipulation that if George ever got back into business, that Lou would give him divisions of his orchid plants to get started.

Mom chuckles now as she recalls thinking the reason for George's visit was to try to match her up with his twenty-one-year-old son, Allen. But he asked Mom to go for a drive with him that afternoon. They went to Fairmount Park and spent a wonderful afternoon talking and enjoying each other. Mom said he was so easy to talk to. She just knew he was "the one."

Mom and Dad planned to get married the following April. However, one Thursday in early December, Dad called Mom on the telephone and said, "Would you want to get married sooner?"

"How soon?" Mom said.

"How about Monday?" Dad said.

They rode to Elkton, Maryland, on Monday, December 8, 1947, (because Maryland didn't require a blood test.) Grandma and "Aunt Floss" Newbourgh, a good friend of Dad's family, went with them as their witnesses. Mom wore a pale pink suit that had scalloped edges on the jacket neckline and hem. Before traveling to Elkton, they had lunch at the Crystal Tea Room in Philadelphia; Mom had oyster soup. At one o'clock in the afternoon they were married in the living room of the house of a local pastor in Elkton. The only thing Mom regrets is that they have no pictures of their wedding day.

Mom gets to her feet and hobbles into her bedroom. She returns and hands me a folded piece of paper. I open the six by eight-inch sheet. I read the pale green stately writing at the top:

Waldorf Astoria Hotel

301 Park Avenue

New York City

The receipt reads: December 10, 1947

2 nights @ $15.75

Total: $31.50

At their first dinner as husband and wife, Mom wore a black velvet dress. She also wore a diamond locket Dad had given her and a white orchid corsage. They were serenaded during dinner by a strolling troubadour.

I give the receipt back to Mom and she looks at it, seeing more than the written words. Her eyes are envisioning the loving husband and lavish surroundings that began their life journey together. As she sits back down, she says her marriage to Dad was another liminal moment in her life.

Mom and Dad shared more than their love; they shared their faith in God. Mom admits it wasn't easy raising grown children who were almost her own age. She understood that she could never replace the mother they lost. But she loved them and showed them that love and kindness.

Mom and Dad had four children of their own, three boys and a girl: Walt, Bill, Ida Ruth, and George. Grandma delivered all of them, except my Bill. Dad delivered Bill "because he came quick!" Grandma couldn't get there soon enough. He always said: "Bill, I was the first one to lay eyes on you."

Dad did start a new business, growing orchids. Uncle Lou's promise to give Dad divisions of his prized plants never materialized. Not to be deterred, Dad started his business with only the back bulbs of old orchid plants. These would have to be grown three years to produce any flowers. In the meantime, Dad grew violets and sold them to flower shops in Atlantic City. Mom worked with him. After three years, Dad grew only orchids. He built two greenhouses and named the business Waldor Orchids. Bill and his brother Walt still run the business today, with eight greenhouses. Mom still pots orchids there and she can't wait to get back to work once she's on her feet again.

Mom and Dad had a good life together. It was not without trials and sorrows; but it was not without joy and laughter either. Dad passed away on April 17, 1987, after a brief illness. Mom cared for him in their home. They were married almost forty years.

I ask Mom if she had a motto she lived by. She slowly rubs her hands together on her lap, then fingers the red blanket. She softly says, "I've tried to live the Golden Rule. I know I haven't always succeeded, but—" She bows her head in thought, then smiles at me with that twinkle in her eye that shows she knows something I don't. "Yes, 'Do unto others as you would have them do unto you.' I have faith that God will help me to do just that."

Then Mom throws back the red blanket, gets up, and hobbles toward the kitchen. She turns, smiles, and says,

"Now, how about some coffee and warm chocolate chip squares with vanilla ice cream?"

I told you there is something wonderful about her.

*   *   *

I never talked to Mom about her heartache over her son George. He struggled for more than twenty years with addiction. He had a few part-time jobs at different places besides our business; he lived with friends; he moved to Florida and went to a rehab there; he lived with friends in Florida; then he moved north and lived with Mom again; and then he met a companion. She helped him sign up for federal assistance and George seemed to be back to his former happy self, settled and resigned to be content with his life.

One January day in 2002, I was helping Bill at the greenhouse when Bill received a call from the local hospital. George was brought into the emergency room and had designated Bill as the person the doctor should speak to. He was not well. He had cirrhosis of the liver. The doctor gave it to Bill straight: George had about three months to live.

George stayed in the hospital for a week or so, then he was moved to a nursing home. Bill and I visited him a few times while he was there. He seemed like his old self, talking, laughing, and caring about us and our kids. He looked better than we had seen him look in years, even though he was in a hospital bed.

In April, George signed himself out of the nursing home and went home to live with his girlfriend at her house in Cape May. One week later, George died in his sleep. He passed away exactly three months, to the very day, after that January phone call from the doctors to Bill.

I know in my heart that Mom never stopped praying for Georgie. Maybe she didn't understand God's plan for him, she never said; but she accepted it because she knew God's plan for all of us is just. Through all those years, she was a pillar of her faith; *even though we questioned her decisions a lot,* she never wavered.

You Gotta Love This Kid

I'm a special education assistant at the local high school. Today has been a hectic day. My last class had a disgruntled and defiant student who shouted obscenities and wouldn't listen or do his work. The commotion set off the other special education students in the class, and the teacher and I had to take all the students, except the shouter, to another classroom. Counsellors were brought in to deal with the shouter. He was eventually escorted to the principal's office by security.

I arrive a bit late to study hall class. It's a large class and I try to smile as I take the roll quickly. Most of the students are busy with homework; some quietly talk to their neighbor.

I see Dylan smile at me in the back of the room as I make my way through the rows of desks.

"Did it hurt?" he asks me.

"Did what hurt?" I ask blankly as I look him in the eye. A lock of brown hair falls across his forehead.

"Did it hurt when you fell from heaven?"

"Huh?"

Then I laugh out loud, smile, and start to giggle. The girls in the back of the class laugh too.

The anxiety of the morning dissolves in the twinkling of his blue eyes. He flicks his hair back. I see a flash of white as he grins and turns to his work.

I smile again.

Thank you, Dylan. You made my day.

Scratch

I wonder what I will be when I grow up. Yes, I laugh at that too, especially at my age. But I press on to do something more, something I'm good at. Hmmmm. My mentors have challenged me, speakers have enlightened me, and my family has encouraged me to try to succeed at what God has helped me accomplish. But still, I wonder . . .

$$* \qquad * \qquad *$$

I know one thing that I will never be: a great baker. I realized that many years ago while I was raising our children.

I would make a vanilla or chocolate cake (my family never liked the odd flavors like carrot cake or lemon). I would get out the General Electric stand mixer that I got as a wedding gift, a couple of eggs, Wesson oil, and a measuring cup. Then, I'd zip open the Duncan Hines box mix and dump it into the bowl.

"Crack, bloink—crack, bloink," went the eggs into the bowl, along with the splash of oil, and a cup or so of water. I'd turn on the mixer and it would whirr the batter around for a few minutes, sending up this whiff of creamy-yumminess. I'd pour the ribbon-like batter into a greased and floured

Bundt pan and pop it into the oven. Thirty-five minutes later, Voila! I had a beautiful cake.

In another hour or so, I'd run a knife around the edge and center funnel of the pan, then flip it over onto a large plate. All over the top and sides of the cake I'd slather an entire can of chocolate frosting, making sure I used a spatula to get every bit of that double-dark chocolatey goodness out of the can.

Ahhhhhh, a perfect cake! It made me proud. Sometimes I'd even toss some colored sprinkles on the top; the kids loved that, and Bill did too.

However, my happiness at seeing my husband and children eat my cake was often dashed to smithereens. One of my "well-meaning" relatives would always pooh-pooh my using a cake mix and canned frosting.

"My kids love homemade cakes; I make mine from scratch," she'd say. (Yet her children were sitting there eating my cake-mix creation.)

I would sit and listen to her rave about the wholesomeness of baking from scratch. I'd heard this before.

She *is* great at baking! Her cakes are delicious! But so are mine! I just take a short-cut to get there.

It takes a lot for me to make goodies—from a box, that is. "Scratch" cakes are even more work and time-consuming. I have tried to make a cake from flour, sugar, butter, and stuff. But oy vey! They turned out terrible. They never tasted like hers . . . ever! It seems she can whip up a scrumptious "scratch" cake with no trouble at all and have it turn out perfectly! She **just might be *the* best baker** in our family.

I am not.

I guess I am jealous of her talent.

Well, later that week, I'm still thinking about my box-mix cakes. They are not really that bad. Why does this homemade stuff bug me? I went to the dictionary to see exactly what "scratch" meant. Here are a few definitions of "scratch" from Mr. Webster.

- To tear or dig with the nails or claws
- **To score no points**
- To manage to get by
- **To gather or scrape together with difficulty**
- An entry withdrawn from a contest
- A hasty mark, scribble
- Put together in haste without much selection
- From the starting line
- Up to standard, acceptable good
- To rub skin lightly
- **To strike out**

Okay, so which "scratch" does our family baker use to make her sugary "scratch" delights?

To me, "scratch" signals disaster.

When I was about twelve years old, I made a chocolate cake from scratch. I creamed the butter and sugar, and measured flour, salt, baking powder, and melted two squares of chocolate over a double boiler, which took forever. Then I baked the chocolatey goo in two round pans.

It smelled so good, but my ego plummeted when my brother Scottie said, "Ooooh, good, brownies!"

My hard work resulted in a one-inch-high layer cake!

That "scratch" cake followed the definition of **"to score no points."**

But I tried homemade baking again, not to be outdone by my relative. This time I made homemade icing, a chocolate frosting I cooked on the stove. After cooling it, I iced the cake. While serving it at a birthday party, the layers slid right off each other! There was an overflowing sea of cake and chocolate icing all over the tablecloth that drew hoots and hollers from my kids and guests! That definition of "scratch" was definitely **"to scrape or gather with difficulty."**

My final relationship with homemade scratch baking was triggered after a Sunday visit with elderly friends. Bill and I were at their home for lunch and treated to homemade bread and rolls at their dining room table. They were delicious, with gobs of butter that just melted away on the warm breads. The hostess extoled the goodness of homemade bread. She also assured me, "It's **so easy** to work with yeast."

Once again, I was duped.

A few weeks later, on a warm fall day, when the kids and their neighborhood friends were playing kickball in our front yard, I made soft pretzels.

I mixed a package of yeast in warm water, added flour, sugar, salt, and whatever else the recipe called for. I put the mixture aside and let the yeast rise, then rolled the dough out, twisted it into pretzels, sprinkled some salt on them, and baked them.

"Kids, I baked some pretzels for you!" I said as I took the cookie sheet of golden pretzels outside. I smiled, and started to gloat to myself, "Move over, Betty Crocker!"

The kids grabbed the warm goodies off the pan, and I went back inside. There was only one left. I was just about to take a bite when I felt a furry body rub against my legs. I looked down into two brown eyes of Molly, our dog.

"Oh, you want a treat too?" I asked. I smiled and patted her head. Molly gave me her left paw. I laughed and gave her the last pretzel.

The next morning when I came home from taking the kids to school, I saw a piece of trash under the yew bush. It was a pretzel. I found another one in the marigolds, and a smashed one by the lamp post! Later that day I even found one in the mailbox! After school, I asked the kids about the pretzels.

"Yeah, Mom, they were terrible," Greg said.

"Shhh, Greg, don't tell her that," Wendy said.

I laughed . . . sorta; then I brought out some Oreo cookies for our snack.

But the final straw came when I found one of my pretzels on the floor of my bedroom closet: Molly wouldn't eat it either!

I achieved the last definition of scratch: **"to strike out"**!

I even struck out with the dog.

Well, lady, guess what?

You win! I surrender. You *are **THE*** great baker of the family!

I resign.

I'm done "scratchin'." Boxed cake mixes, here I come! Canned icing, "I love you." Frozen soft pretzels, come fill my freezer!

Bill laughed when I told him about the pretzels that evening, then he had the guts to grab a bag of pretzel sticks and head to the den to watch TV with the kids.

Okay, Lord, the pretzel thing was funny, but how come I still feel like a failure because I can't bake like others do? I feel like I'm only good for a laugh.

The next morning, I called my mother. She laughed so hard at my pretzel story you would think I was a stand-up comic.

"That's so funny! Those kids and that dog, I love them!" she said. I could hear her teacup clatter in its saucer.

"Mom, it's *not that* funny!"

"Oh, will you forget about baking from scratch! Folks are good at all kinds of things. But *baking is not your talent.* That is for others. You have better things to do, anyway," she said.

"Yeah, like what?" I twirled the red phone cord around and around like a jump rope. Maybe I shouldn't have called my mother.

"You can do *anything* you put your mind to," she said. I heard a teaspoon ping against her cup.

"Yeah, like what?" I said in a whisper. I gnawed on my lip. I wrote Bill's name in the dust on the end table.

"Why don't you paint with oils, or work at a bank, learn to ice skate, go to school, become a teacher, or a great writer." She rattled off the list as fast as lightening. Then she added, "Don't be kidded, **God has great things He wants you to do.** You just must reach out in faith and trust Him to lead the way."

My ears perked up. I straightened my shoulders.

Yes, God *has* things for me to do, *great things*!

I looked at the end table; the dust didn't look so thick. I spun the cord on the wall phone even faster.

Mother always had a way of making me feel better.

I guess that's what mother's do best.

*   *   *

Mother was right, again. God did have great plans for me.

The following summer I passed the entrance exam to the local community college. That fall I began my college journey; I went to night classes, studying writing every semester from September 1992 until May 2012.

Lord, I'm not and will never be a great baker; and I'm okay with that.

But maybe if I follow You and take Your hand, You will help me be a worthy writer, just for Mother.

Something Simple

I make cloth napkins. I use fabric pieces called "fat quarters." These are squares of fabric precut into eighteen-by twenty-one-inch squares used by quilters. I'm picky about the fabric they're made of though. It must be soft yet hold its shape.

There are six napkins in a set. Every set is all the same color with different white designs. Each of the six napkins is a different pattern: some have polka dots, some flowers, some geometric shapes, some stripes. They are pretty and perky. I have made these sets in turquoise, red, blue, coral, black, yellow, and purple.

I pin the frayed edges under and stitch around the four sides with my sewing machine.

"Whirrrr!"

I love that sound. It's pleasant and smooth; the gears go round, the needle goes up and down, and the fabric moves forward. (How does it do that so effortlessly, when all I do is press the foot pedal?)

Sewing these napkins takes time. Time to pin every edge. Time to sew around them. Time to think. Not to think about what I am doing, but to pause from the busy-ness of my day and slow down, to do something simple: to "be still" and to think.

Yes, that's the best part, it makes me "be still." God tells us to, "Be still and know that I am God." I forget that a lot. I'm up early to go to the school where I work. I come home, walk the dog, grocery shop, do laundry, phone the kids, check on a neighbor, cook, do paperwork, go to bed, and repeat the same thing again the next day. I am not still, and my mind is not still.

Then I squeeze in time to sew some simple napkins.

I put my sewing machine on the dining room table, open my box of pins with the big colored pearls on the end of each one, and I pin edges and sew around and around.

I find a calm come over me. It's God's gift to me; my mind is at peace.

I give these finished, pressed cloth napkins to friends and family. I do get strange looks from the receiver. They seem to say, "What am I going to do with these?"

"Ha!"

I don't know if they will be used or not. But with each one, I give a little bit of myself. Maybe when they're setting a table, or even mopping their chin, I hope these simple napkins will bring beauty to their table and a smile to their face.

Mickey's Done It Again

"*H*ow'd he, do it? How *did* he do it?" Bill asks me, shaking his head. His bright blue eyes give me that incredulous look of unbelief.

"I don't know," I say, feeling the skin on my ribs jiggle as I stifle a giggle.

"That's impossible to do!" Bill shakes his head again. "He ate all the peanut butter! All of it! I had it smeared into all the nooks and crannies of that fake piece of cheese. It's gone! And so is he!"

I smile and laugh aloud. "You're so funny, Bill!"

"No, now I'm really, really, mad. Wait 'til tomorrow. You'll see! Mickey's gonna get it!"

"You're a crazy man, but I love you!" I smile, and I see him smile amid his frustration. He sits down and butters his toast.

"You've been trying to catch that mouse for three days now. He's outsmarted you every time." I laugh out loud.

Bill looks at me and takes a bite of toast, then stirs his coffee.

"Debby, look. I set the trap, put it on the floor. Then, I barely touch it with my sleeve and the trap springs! How can he eat everything on that trap, even in the tiny holes of that plastic cheese, and not get caught?" He looks away, seemingly devising his next move.

"I don't know, hon, but I love you." I smile again, give him a hug, and get ready for work.

Choices

I put the last of the bags in the car and close the back gate. The market was crowded today. I back my car out of the parking spot and a car is already waiting to take my spot. Mid-afternoon on a hot July day was not the ideal time to go grocery shopping. I wonder if I got all the items on my shopping list—the list that I left at home on the kitchen table. I steer my car out of the parking lot, down the short road to the main street.

As I drive on, I see an old man on a beat-up bicycle riding next to me to my right. He has two full yellow plastic grocery bags swinging, one on each handlebar. Just as I pass him, both bags break open! Canned goods, apples, a head of lettuce, and boxes crash and roll on the black top. The car behind me swerves. I drive forward through the green light as I watch the man in my rearview mirror. He hops off his bike with both hands to his head, looks around, then looks up in the air, seemingly searching for an answer. Then he scratches his beard and shakes his head.

"What's that man going to do?" I ask aloud. I can't stop looking. Suddenly, I glanced to my right and see two green canvas bags on the passenger seat of my car.

I can give them to him!!

I stop at the stop sign and turn right. But then I must stop because cars are backed up to the next traffic light. I realize that I'd have to go around the big city block once I got through this light, stop at two more traffic lights, and wait at a left-hand turn. By the time I got back, the man would be gone.

The light turns green, and I go straight.

Straight home to my house.

For days, weeks, and months after that, I feel terrible. I'm so embarrassed! How could I not have helped that poor man when I could have done so? I didn't even try!

Oh Lord! I'm supposed to be a servant of Yours, and I failed that man, and I failed You!

Humph . . . a fine example of my faith, aren't I?

Please forgive me Lord . . . please?

That afternoon haunted me for months. I couldn't get it out of my mind.

*   *   *

Landon, my labrador retriever, jumps onto the back seat of the car. He is anxious to go for a ride. Today, it is to Long-port Beach, about three miles away. It is a cloudy, cold, windy November afternoon. We drive through town and head over the Somers Point-Longport causeway.

I speed up as I approach the high-arching bridge that goes over the intercoastal waterway. Halfway up the bridge I see an elderly lady riding against traffic on an old bike on the shoulder of the other lane. She struggles to pedal her bike up the high expanse against the cold, strong wind. Her tan coat flaps in the wind and she has its hood pulled tight around her face.

I zero in on the two full, yellow plastic shopping bags swinging on her handlebars.

Is this déjà vu?

"Okay, Lord, I'm ready this time!"

I step on the gas, go up, over, and down the bridge. At the light at the base of the bridge I make a U-turn, then I pull over and wait on the side of the road. Eventually, I see her coming. I get out of my car as she flies down the bridge on the shoulder of the road.

I flail my arms in the air and jump up and down, flagging her down. She scrapes her high-top black sneakers on the gravel until she stops. The bike tips sideways with the weight and swing of the bags, but she catches the handlebars before it falls to the ground.

I smile at her, motion, and say, "You need help!"

"What?" she asks as she pulls the hood off her head and cups her ear. Her gray hair is tousled in the wind.

"I said, you need help!" Then I smile at her.

"No, I don't," she says quietly, with a smirk. Over the top of her glasses, her brown eyes peek at me. She swipes her windblown hair off her face. Then she turns a bit sideways and looks at me through her heavy lenses like I am from Mars.

"Yes, you do need help," I say. "Those bags are going to break!" As I speak to her, I take one yellow, plastic bag and drop it into my green canvas bag. As I hang it on her handlebar I notice its contents: cans of cat food.

"Really, I'm fine," she protests softly as I fill the other green bag and slide it on her other handlebar.

I smile at her.

She smiles too.

"What's your name?" I ask.

She looks me in the eye and cocks her head to the left.

Again, I said, "What's your name?" I smile and see she heard me this time.

"Oh, it's Francis," she said as she scuffs the gravel with her toe.

"Glad to meet you, Francis. I'm Debby," I say.

She leans forward and brushes the hair from her ear.

"Where are you coming from Francis?"

"I work at the McDonald's in Somers Point, but I had to go to the grocery store after work today," she says.

"Gee, that's two miles from here ... and where do you live?" The wind catches my breath.

"Huh?" She tips her head sideways.

"Where are you going, Francis?"

"Atlantic City," she says as she points north with her gloved hand.

"Atlantic City! Francis, that's ten miles from here!" I yell in disbelief.

"Yeah, I know, but I do it all the time. It's nothin'," she says as she looks at the horizon, then the ground.

"Francis, let me take you home! I'll put your bike in the back of my car. You can't ride all the way to Atlantic City! Besides, it's getting dark. It's four o'clock!"

"I'm fine, Betty," she says. She rakes her fingers through her hair, then pulls her hood up and ties the string under her chin. She pushes her glasses up on the bridge of her nose, looks at me, and pats her bike.

"It's how I get places; by bike, I mean," she says. "I'm okay, really. Thanks anyway, and for the bags." She looks at me and smiles. I see my reflection in the lenses of her eyeglasses.

She straightens, bangs the rusty kickstand up, and shoves off the gravel.

"Tootles! Bye-bye!" she says, with a quick wave. She struggles hard against the wind as she balances the heavy swinging bags.

"Francis," I call. "Please, let me take you home! It's no trouble!"

She calls over her shoulder, "Thanks, but no thanks. And I promise I won't get in any trouble. Bye!" She gives me a backwards wave as she pedals into the wind.

I turn, then look back, and sigh.

"I tried Lord . . . I really tried this time," I said aloud.

I get in my car. Landon is waiting patiently. We head along the same road that Francis travels. As I pass her, I slow down, open my window, and yell, "Are you sure, Francis?"

She turns, smiles, and waves me on with a flourish of her hand.

Giants

*G*iants.

The twelve Israelite spies saw giants when they entered the Promised Land. When they returned to Moses, ten of the Israelite spies were afraid of the Promised Land. They told Moses and the Israelites that the people were gigantic! Those giants were descendants of Anak and they were huge, strong people. "We were like grasshoppers in their sight."

However, Joshua and Caleb, the other two Israelite spies, showed Moses and the people the bountiful fruit they brought back from the Promised Land. They said it was just as God had said, "the land flowing with milk and honey." The land God had promised them. Caleb and Joshua believed they could overcome the giants with God's help.

Fear and unbelief won. Moses and the Israelites chose not to enter the Promised Land.

The Israelites failed to trust the Lord's promise; they failed to believe Joshua and Caleb. They were afraid of the gigantic people who were there. So, because of the Israelite's unbelief, God allowed them to wander in the wilderness for forty years, until that entire unbelieving generation was gone.

*　　　*　　　*

I, too, see giants in my life. I struggle with what I see, and what I know that God has promised me.

Each time one of our children has graduated high school, the phenomenal price of college looms in front of me like a giant. I feel like one of the Israelites facing the giants and begin to question how we will ever pay those costs. Not only the price of education for our two children who are now in college, but for our other three children as well.

Giants.

Big, twenty-first-century giants frighten me. They loom before me. I worry. I flounder. I try and I fail.

Then, I open my Bible, in faith, and claim His promises to me.

I trust; because when I trust, I succeed.

I believe that our children were given the ability to get into the schools of their choice and the opportunity to study at the nation's finest schools. The Lord has taken them this far; I must trust and face the giants that are before me and believe that these giants are not so big for a God so great.

Then, a scholarship is awarded; a raise is given to my husband; and I find myself back in the work force. I now have a job I like, one that gets me home by three o'clock for our children when they get out of school. These changes were not because of any great thing that Bill or I had done, but because God has blessings to pour out on His faithful people.

I try, and I fail; I trust, and I succeed.

Giants are scary. They come in many different forms these days. However, my God is the same yesterday, today, and forever.

Ethel and Thelma

I cleaned houses for many years. Yup, other people's dirt was my money. It was hard, exhausting, thankless work. I would clean up to three houses a day. It was a lonely job where your thoughts could wander and your self-esteem plummet. But we had five children, and housekeeping helped put our children through college. The money was good, so I did it.

I also put *myself* through college during all those years of tuition payments. I knew I didn't want to be housekeeping ten years down the road. So, when our oldest child started college and our youngest started first grade, I started at the community college. At thirty-seven years old, I was always the oldest student in my class. Then I went to Rowan University and majored in communications with a specialization in writing. I did like to write, and still do.

Changeovers were a "crapshoot." Those were weekly rentals along the shore that had to be cleaned when vacationers ended their week. I had less than two hours to clean each place before the next guest arrived. You never knew if the renters would leave a place that just needed a "once over" good cleaning, or if they would leave a refrigerator full of week-old food, soda spilt on the floor, shag carpet and all, and a bathroom where someone ran and barfed, missing the hopper. I would tell myself this would make a good story; you can't make this stuff up. Luckily, the good changeovers outweighed the bad. I woke early to clean these gems, week after week all season long. Then, I'd clean another one or two houses after that—all before the two o'clock Saturday arrival time for new guests. It was a fast paced, lonely job.

However, there were other clients whose houses I kept, and I became like part of their family—a sometimes seen, sometimes unseen, family member.

I recall especially two old-lady sisters, Thelma and Ethel, who lived in a small house in Ocean City, New Jersey, along with their two cats. I cleaned their house every other Wednesday. Thelma had Alzheimer's and never spoke to me. But Ethel was so happy to have someone to talk to. When I was there, she often chattered non-stop the entire time, following me from room to room.

Their house was a housekeeper's nightmare. Their furniture was old, with slipcovers that had to be straightened once the cat hair was vacuumed off. They had every souvenir made of seashells ever made; and every knick-knack they ever had was displayed on floor-to-ceiling shelves. Nestled among these shelves were nubs of candles that had been used ten years ago. Those shelves also held Christmas bric-a-brac that was too much trouble to put away after the holidays, so it stayed out all year long. Ethel reminded me often about living through the Depression. If she ever needed money, she could sell her "stuff" and not starve. I get why she kept everything.

Between dusting those shelves, sweeping cat litter up off the linoleum, and cleaning two bathrooms used by two old ladies who must have had diarrhea an awful lot, the worst job was vacuuming the carpets. It just so happened that the Wednesdays I cleaned for the old girls, the local podiatrist came early in the day to tend to their feet. He did his work in the living room as the ladies sat on the sagging davenport. The toenails of twenty toes must have been flying, as the old olive-green living room rug was covered with yellowed, hard clippings. I would run the vacuum over them, but the rugs were so threadbare that those darn toenail shards would get caught in the ragged fibers. I would end up having to dig them out with my fingernails. (I don't even know if I ever told my kids I did that.) I recall telling myself, you should write about "housekeeping" when you get home. But I was always too darn tired at the end of the day to write anything.

The last time I was at Ethel and Thelma's house, Thelma (the one who never spoke) ran into the kitchen shouting, "Please, help my sister!" I looked in surprise, then I ran to the living room and found Ethel. She had fallen out the front door (she probably missed the step) and was lying, flat-out and dazed, on the concrete lanai. She was a good-sized woman, and I didn't try to lift her. I ran back into the living room and gathered a small, tattered pillow from the sofa and put it under her head. I covered her with an afghan to keep her warm. She argued with me when I told her I had to call 911. But I did just that.

Along with other reasons for not wanting to move her, Ethel had her left arm in a cast. She had broken it two weeks before, dishing ice cream. I stayed with her until the paramedics and her son arrived.

While Ethel was sprawled out on the concrete porch, Thelma was in her own little world, singing and holding one cat so he wouldn't run away.

The EMTs agreed that Ethel was okay, but that she and Thelma shouldn't be living by themselves. While the paramedics talked to Jim, her son, I held her hand and told her I loved her as she lay on her bed in her room. Although her blue eyes had lost their sparkle, she squeezed my hand, smiled briefly, and said, "I love you, too."

I hugged her. Then I put my cleaning stuff in my car and left; I was exhausted. I recall glancing at their house again as I turned the corner saying, "Did all that just happen? And again, you can't make this stuff up!"

Two weeks later, Ethel died of bone cancer; hence the broken arm from dishing ice cream. I went to her funeral. Jim, his wife Diane, two others, and I were the only ones there. I laid a small bouquet of orchids in the casket; she liked flowers.

Thelma was now in a nursing home.

Not long after that, I hung up my duster for good.

Who Does That?

Very often at night, my husband, Bill, and I will take a walk. Sometimes it is to the causeway that links Somers Point to Ocean City, New Jersey. The causeway is a raised road above the marshland with high-arching bridges at each end. It's a beautiful 2.8-mile road with the two spans: one across the intercoastal waterway and the other across the bay. In between the high-arching bridges the road is as flat as the bay and its marsh grasses. This new causeway was built within the last two decades. A walk along the concrete footpath next to the road is beautiful during the day because its height allows one to gaze at the boats in the waterways, and to see the Atlantic Ocean over the island of Ocean City. But in the evening, it is even more beautiful.

A large, stately information center and parking lot are located before the high bridge into Ocean City. Bill parks the car there. Now, during the summertime, the raucous sound of birds fills the air. We walk to the railing along the concrete walkway that overlooks Cowpen Island. This island is filled with trees, bushes, and marsh grasses. At this time of year there are hundreds of birds there: great blue herons, white herons, egrets, black ibis, white ibis, yellow crowned night herons, laughing gulls, herring gulls, and red-winged blackbirds. It is a calliope of beautiful birds in song. They flap their wings and stretch their necks, calling for their mates to come sit on the nest with them. Then some take off in search of food or twigs to add to their nest. We get there after our dinner and before the sun sets. The birds are homing into their nests. It is a bird sanctuary like no other! The noise of their cries and flapping of wings fills the air. Other folks line up along the railing, some with cameras that have telescopic lenses a foot long. The sky turns orange and peach, the clouds a dusky purple, as the cries of the birds grow louder. They fly close above our heads and land on high branches or in the thicket where their nests and mates are. The sun falls past the horizon. Drifters flap their wings and come in for a landing, squawking as if to say, "I'm finally here!"

Bill and I leave the railing and start our walk. We don't walk the entire bridge, but head towards Somers Point, facing the darkening sky of the setting sun. The bird sounds are quieter the further we go.

We hold hands. We talk softly to each other.

A runner passes us.

After a quarter mile, we come to an out-cropping on the bridge. We stop and look over the rail at the choppy, dark bay. A few whitecaps raise their heads as a stiff wind picks up. The waves stand out as the darkness of the evening sets in, but the coolness of the breeze feels good. We continue our relaxing walk until we overlook the fishing pier below. Fishermen are casting their rods; I guess fishing is better in the dark. Then we turn and head back to our car.

*   *   *

Tonight, however, we go for a different walk, along a marina at the bay. We park the car in the small lot along Bay Avenue.

"Take your hat and gloves," I say to Bill as I pull on my own.

The night is very dark. There is no moon in the sky. A stiff cold wind blows and catches my breath. I turn and take Bill's gloved hand. We walk the five blocks along the dark road to the bay. There are no streetlights. I turn up my collar against the wind. To our left is a marina of boats—the die-hards left in the water during the off season. The dark, choppy water laps against these cocooned sailboats and cabin cruisers both large and small. There are no bright lights tonight, only the dim glow of the lamps at the end of a few docks. The wind blows through halyards on raised masts with an eerie sound. The boats are wintering—dark, closed up, some hooded from the elements.

On the other side of this narrow road is a boatyard, where huge boats are dry-docked, close together. Their rigs rise high above us, the massive boats shrouded in white plastic, sucked into every side to keep the weather at bay. If I wasn't in my hometown, I would be frightened by the stillness of the dark marina to my left and hooded boats to my right. It's spooky tonight. No one is around, only me, Bill, the wind, and the waves.

Bill and I arrive at the end of the road and look at high tide over the low railing. The waves go in and out, flicking back spray when the wind catches them.

"The clouds are low tonight," Bill says as he points a gloved hand to Ocean City across the bay on the horizon. The lights of the city look fuzzy because of those clouds. We stay there for a long time, not needing any words. The cold sets in. The windsock at the end of the far pier sticks out straight and spins with the contrary gusts. We turn to go back to the car. I quicken my pace.

"Bill," I say, "I really have to pee."

He catches up to me and tugs my sleeve. Even though I can only make out his profile and the darkness of his features, I can see his jaw drop.

"We're only two miles from home," he says.

"Yeah, I know. But I gotta go." I'm starting to jiggle, and then he knows I'm not kidding.

"Well, run over to that Port-A-Potty over there, I'll wait. Hurry!" Then he adds, "Let me hold your gloves. I'm going to look at the boats over there."

I toss him the gloves and race to the johnny-on-the-spot. The door creaks open, then bangs shut. Even though it's pitch black, I zing down my zipper, spin around, and do the helicopter hover over the toilet as I'm just about ready to burst. I feel relief right away as the surging of my bladder matches the waves outside.

"Wait!!!...Wait!!!.... What's going on? What's happening??"

The back of my jeans is getting soaked! A warm stream is flowing down the back of my legs into my shoes.   Is   this thing overflowing?

"Arrg!" I scream.

"Debby? You, okay?" I hear Bill call from a distance.

What do I do? Do I stop mid-stream? Or just let it rip? I can't see a thing. I turn to look behind me and see nothing but blackness. The cuffs of my jeans wick up puddles from the floor.

I scream, "Is this thing overflowing?"

"Are you okay?" Bill asks again, closer this time.

"Bill, I'm all wet! I don't know what's going on. This thing must have overflowed. Stuff is splashing everywhere!" I scream.

I feel for the roll of paper and wipe, which is just ridiculous. I fling the paper behind me. My socks squish into my shoes as I try to pull my wet jeans up in the dark. I open the door and Bill grabs my hand and helps me out of the miry pit.

"What in the world happened?" Bill asks, staring at my akimbo stance, unzipped pants, and cowboy-like walk as though I've been in the saddle too long.

"Oh, I don't know, I'm soaked through! My jeans are freezing to my legs!"

Suddenly, I stop.

I turn and straddle back. I fling johnny's door open wide. The dock lights allow in just enough light, and I peer inside.

"You're kidding me! **Who does that?!**" I scream.

"Arrrggh!" I scream again and flail my arms up and down as I slam the door and waddle, half frozen, to Bill, shouting again, **"Who does that?"**

"Who does **WHAT?**" Bill pumps his hands up and down, motioning me to keep quiet and calm down.

It doesn't work.

"Who puts the lid down on a Port-A-Potty??!!!"

I spin around and march ahead of him—stomp, squish, stomp, squish. My legs and tush are like ice, my jeans stiff as a board. I am almost in tears.

I open the car door, throw the rubber floor mat on the seat, and crawl in like a beached whale.

Bill gets in.

We go home in silence.

At home, I open the car door and roll off the seat. Bill takes my hand, and I do the Frankenstein walk up the path and front steps. Then, in unison we turn, look at each other and say:

"Who does that?!!"

Bill laughs out loud.

I am not amused. I turn and glare at him. He motions to zipper his mouth, but it is not working; his cheeks are puffed out, his belly bouncing up and down, and those blue eyes of his have that sparkle.

I stare and shout, "It's not funny!"

He tries to hide behind his glove. Then he throws his head back and laughs out loud like he's at a hilarious comedy show.

I tromp inside.

"Who does that?!!" I shout again.

"It's not funny!"

Then again ... **maybe it is.**

Ol' Blue in My Kitchen

Ol' Blue is a colander in my kitchen.

He's a large, blue metal bowl covered in small holes in diamond designs. One metal handle hangs loose; a screw is missing. and two of his three metal feet are gone. Ol' Blue is bent here and there, and some of the blue enamel has chipped off, worn from years of dinners, picnics, and good meals for my husband, our five children, and me.

But I keep him. He has strained mounds of spaghetti, rotini, and pasta of every kind, and vegetables, too—spinach, lettuce, and green beans to name a few.

I take Ol' Blue for granted. He resides in the bottom kitchen cupboard, sandwiched between the four-quart and six-quart stainless steel pots. He waits sometimes for days, even weeks, until I reach for him.

But I can count on Ol' Blue when I need him.

During the summer months I grab Ol' Blue and head out to the garden. I pull up carrots, onions, beets, and lettuce and fill Ol' Blue's deep bowl. I'll thump Blue hard on the cinderblock wall, and dirt from these goodies falls through his holes in a soft mound. I trek inside and plop Ol' Blue in the kitchen sink, splash cool water on the entire bowl, give him a good shake to get all the dribbles of water out, then toss

Blue's harvest with a swish-plunk into a large ceramic bowl. I head back out to the garden and fill him to overflowing again with string beans and tomatoes. Once again, I "thump" Ol' Blue on the wall, leaving another mound of soil, then head back to the kitchen and repeat.

This beat-up old colander seems to have a rhythm of his own: a **"thump"** on the wall, **"plop"** in the sink, **"splash"** of water, **"shake"** the **"dribble"** of trickling water, and the finale—a **"swish-plunk"** of the veggies falling into the bowl.

"Thump, plop, splash, shake, dribble, swish-plunk!"

If Ol' Blue could talk, he would puff out his round blue bowl, put his handle in the air and sing that jazzy tune out loud and say, "Who else in the cupboard can do what I do?"

No one, little colander, no one!

I put Ol' Blue in soapy water and rub the sponge all over him, both inside and out, and rinse him under clear, cool water. A terry cloth towel wicks away any drops of water left. Then I open the cupboard door and sandwich him once again between the four-quart and six-quart pots. His handle sticks up in the air as though he's waving good-bye.

Ol' Blue and I have a special bond. He's old and worn.

Yes, we're a lot alike.

However, he is too much a part of me, my family, and my life to part with him.

I smile and close the cupboard door. Until next time, my friend.

The Little Things

*T*he sun has faded. Through the small window the pink sky is mixing with the gray of the darkening day, bare branches are still visible against the changing sky. It's quiet here at the university library. I need the quiet. In quietness, and in the little things, the Lord reveals what is most precious to Him. I know that. But all too often, I am too busy to be still.

I love the stories in the Bible where God takes the weak and makes them strong; where He takes the little and glorifies His name; where He takes the few and makes them abundant; where He takes the quiet and re-sounds their story two thousand years later.

Most of us want to be acknowledged, patted on the back, thanked, thought of as being useful to someone, or that what we do is worthwhile. But it doesn't happen like that; we often go un-thanked, are overlooked, or passed by. We put in our time doing seemingly meaningless things that no one cares about. But those meaningless things leave bits of ourselves for those who come behind us.

I go through my day at work, at school, at home, and I can't see how I'm making any difference in anyone's life. I must remind myself that God works in those who do the little things for Him. Those who do the meaningless, thankless, selfless things are His kingdom builders.

Kingdom builders are the people who, you realize in hindsight, showed you what God's love is all about. Kingdom builders lay the foundation of His love for you, in the quietness of their ways.

My dad was a kingdom builder.

My father, Franklin Law, worked at a supermarket chain from the 1940s to the 1960s. He fixed all their refrigerated meat, dairy, and frozen cases. Russ Young, a man from my father's church, got Dad that job in 1945 after Dad got out of the Navy. Dad always called Russ, "The Duke," after the movie star John Wayne, because of Russ's large stature and commanding presence.

In 1963, Russ had a stroke. He was paralyzed. His tiny wife, Helen, took care of him every day, giving him a sponge bath and combing his hair. But even Helen admitted that Russ needed "a good dunking" once a week. He was too big for her to do that.

So, every Tuesday night, after a full day's work, Dad would go over to Russ's apartment and bathe him and wash his hair, lifting him into and out of the bathtub. Dad did this for four years. Nowadays, people would have a home health worker come in to help, but back then there was no such help available, and if there was, they could not have afforded it.

However, Dad did it for his friend.

"I'm going over to The Duke's house," Dad would tell my mother, and off he'd go.

Dad's dedication touched my heart forever. He saw a need and filled it; he saw a job and did it; he loved his friend and showed it. That's what kingdom builders do.

One night while Dad was taking care of Russ, my mother and I had tea with Helen in their small apartment kitchen. I remember Helen brought out her electric frying pan and put it on the kitchen table and turned it on. She went to a kitchen drawer and brought out a handful of clear, colored marbles.

"Wait and see what happens," Helen said. She laughed, and her blue eyes twinkled when she dropped the marbles in the hot pan.

"Ooooh," I said, "I like the blue one, and the yellow, and the green one!"

"Just keep watching," Helen said.

"What's gonna happen?" Mom asked. She smiled, looked at Helen and then at me.

"You'll see."

The marbles started to dance around in the pan, almost like they were jumping across the hot sand at the beach.

After five minutes, Helen turned off the frying pan and dumped the marbles into a bowl of ice water.

"Crack!" went the yellow marble muffled by the water.

"Crack! Crack! Crack! Crack!" the other marbles sounded, one after the other.

"Oooooh, look at them! Mommy, look! Wow!" I said.

Each marble was a work of crackle glass art. The marbles were cracked inside but not broken. They were the most beautiful things my ten-year-old eyes had ever seen.

Helen poured our tea, and as we drank it, she glued a little silver cap on top of the cooled blue marble and put a long white ribbon through the hole in the top of the cap.

"For you," Helen said as she handed me the beautiful blue marble necklace.

"For, me?" I asked. "Thank you!"

Mommy tied the long ribbon around my neck. I fingered the smooth blue marble; the light from the hanging kitchen lamp made all the cracks sparkle. I held the marble up close to my eyeball and closed the other eye. Looking toward the bright light bulb in the lamp, I squinted and saw marbled streaks of light blue, dark blue, and every blue in between. I moved the marble around and it became a kaleidoscope of moving blue patterns. It spun me into a swirling brilliant orbit, like I was viewing the blue earth from a rocket ship.

I got up and looked at my new necklace in the shiny stainless-steel toaster on Helen's counter. I loved it. I felt so grown up and pretty.

"Thank you again," I said as I gave Helen a hug.

"No, thank *you*, thank *you all*, for being here," Helen said as she hugged me tight.

My Dad: the kingdom builder. He was a man of very few words, but his actions spoke volumes.

Little things, like helping a friend get a bath every Tuesday night, or even a small gift of a blue marble, show the power of God at work.

Kingdom builders sprinkle little things into our lives; and if we are quiet enough, and still enough, we'll notice them.

In a Whisper

I have walked with God for a long time. I know Him and He knows me. I pray that my children will love the Lord too. But I don't speak of the Lord often to them. It's like the words will not come forth. My heart is full, yet my words are silent. However, I do always pray with them when they leave; yes, even now at their age. I've done this since they left for their very first day of kindergarten.

It was late August. Abbey and her husband, Walker, just had a beautiful baby boy, named Finn. After our visit with them, Bill, Cami, and I were all saying good-bye to Abbey at their house in Connecticut. I hated to leave Abbey and our new grandson. Finn was only a week old, and they would be so far away from us. We live two hundred miles away in southern New Jersey. I kept thinking, I should pray with Abbey.

But I didn't.

I thought it again as I walked down the porch steps.

But I still didn't. We got in the car and drove away making our way through the narrow tree-lined streets of quaint houses to the highway.

Several miles from Abbey's house I said to Bill, "I have to go back."

"You have to go back, or you just don't want to leave Abbey and Finn?" Bill asked, searching my face with his deep blue eyes.

"I have to go back."

"Really?"

"Yes, I have to," I said, so quietly I could hardly hear myself.

Bill turned the car around and we headed back.

At Abbey's door I rang the bell. She opened the door, and I stepped inside. We looked in each other's eyes; it was like we both knew why I was there. We hugged and cried for what seemed like a long time.

"Abbey, I have to pray with you," I said quietly.

But my words wouldn't come. We hugged for elongated seconds, and finally, the words came … in a whisper:

> … *"Thank you, God, … for Abbey, Walker, … and little Finn. Bless them, Lord, with health and strength and happiness. … Give Abbey and Walker wisdom as they raise Finn, that they would glorify You."*

The prayer was a quiet whisper, like a gossamer thread joining our hearts with the Lord.

The whisper resonated in each of us. The house was quiet, with mother and daughter hugging in the soft afternoon sunlight in the living room. We felt the love of Jesus in that very room, and another whisper of his love in the cradle upstairs.

The Final Gift

I never saw my mother cry. I saw her grieve, I saw her sad, I saw her emotional, but I never saw her cry. My mother had no tears; she just did not. She wore glasses, and only when she reached the age of eighty-nine was she prescribed eye drops for dry eyes. I remember she said to my children when my father died: "People think I am not sad because I'm not crying. My heart is broken in two. I'm crying on the inside. I just don't have any tears to show it."

Sometimes, when we least expect it, the Lord works in mysterious ways to let us know He is with us, telling us that everything is okay and that His eyes are upon us.

*   *   *

For the past month my mother, Margaret, has been in and out of the hospital and rehab. She is in the hospital again, but this time she seems so very frail. I worry. Here at Shore Memorial Hospital, she lies still in her bed. Her room is sunny, with large windows overlooking the Great Egg Harbor Bay, but she doesn't notice the harbor, full of cabin cruisers and white sailboats, or the skyline of Ocean City on the horizon, dominated by the monstrous Ferris wheel at Gillian's Wonderland Pier.

Mother's vision seems limited only to the room she is in, and her visitors, sometimes. She is quiet. She only speaks when spoken to. Now and then, when I think she is asleep, I will look at her and her eyes will be following me around the room as I straighten her get-well cards or gaze out the window. She says nothing. She asks for nothing. She doesn't ask about her health. She is failing, and I think she knows it, though she never mentions it, and neither do I.

I bend over and give her a kiss. I take hold of her hands. They feel like the hands of a sparrow, as light as air and boney, so very fragile and thin. She tries to raise her arms for a hug. I lean over her and hug her with a gentle squeeze. I bury my head in the side of her head, her untamed blonde hair soft against my face. I close my eyes. *Lord, please take care of my mother. She needs Your love and Your strength. Help me to help her in any way I can.*

I smile and pull a chair up next to her bed. I tell her about my job at school and our kids.

"Wendy, Greg, Gavin, and Abbey are all in different states working at their jobs. Cami is at the University of Delaware. Gavin is applying at the University of Missouri for the master's degree program in journalism. They always ask about you, Mom; they love you so much.

"Oh, wow," Mother whispers and smiles. She looks at me and there is a twinkle in her blue eyes; but it quickly fades away. Her smile fades and her gaze wanders over my head. Then, she closes her eyes.

"They're good kids," she finally says, her eyes still closed, yet she smiles. She turns her head on the pillow toward the ceiling.

"Oh, golly yes, Mom. They are all doing what they should be doing," I say with enthusiasm, trying to lighten the mood. "But I miss them."

Mother smiles and runs the back of her hand across her lips and opens her eyes. Then, she drops her hand on the blanket across her chest, exhausted. She turns her head towards me; her questioning blue eyes search mine. I look away trying not to acknowledge her weakness, but she knows I noticed it. She knows she is dying. I do too.

"Mom, would you like a drink of water?" I pour some fresh water into a pink plastic cup. I hold it to her lips, and she takes a few sips then shoos the cup away with the slight raise of her finger. She smiles as I pat her mouth with a clean tissue.

"Thank you," she whispers.

I put the cup on the table beside her bed, walk toward the window and take off my jacket. The sky is blue with white puffy clouds. I set my jacket on the windowsill and turn. Mom's eyes are following me. I smile at her and sit back down in my chair. She smiles back. I hold her hand and tell her about Bill and the greenhouse business; about Wendy who teaches school; Cami's crew team; and Abbey who travels all around the world in her new job. Mother watches me, nods that she understands, and moves her hand in mine. I tell her about Gavin and Greg, how one is in Pennsylvania, the other in Florida, yet they talk to each other frequently. Then I look at Mother again. She's asleep. Her chest rises and falls steadily in long rhythmic breaths; her hand relaxes in mine.

I look out the window at the harbor; I swallow hard because I know I will not have my mother much longer. *Lord, was it just six weeks ago, in early April, that I picked Mother up at her assisted living apartment, bought two hoagies and some sodas, and we went and sat on the bulkhead by the bay? From here I can see the exact place where we sat and ate, at the end of that road, right there, Lord, right there.*

I twist in my chair so Mother won't see my face if she wakes up. I bite my lips. *Lord, that day at the water's edge she looked at me and said, "What would I do without you?" I smiled at her and said, "No, what would I do without you?" Then we laughed together. The tide was high that day. The water splashed in waves against the wooden bulkhead we sat on. Lord, it was beautiful. Lord, she was happy. Lord, I was happy.* The smell of creosote, salt air, and Italian subs wafted in when the wind gusted from the east across the water. Laughing gulls lined up on the pilings of the marina, cawing to each other, their calls echoing through the tall masts and flying bridges of boats rocking in their slips.

I look back at my mother now. She is slipping away from me. I feel the back of my throat swell and tears fill my eyes. Then, I think of Mother's lack of tears. I guess she had tears before my sister, Marilyn, died two years before I was born. I will have to ask my older brothers, Frankie, Ronnie, and Scottie, if they remember Mother crying tears then. The boys were nine, eleven, and thirteen when Marilyn passed away. Kennie and I never knew our sister.

Marilyn died when she was four years old. Childhood diabetes is the cause listed on her death certificate. I know Mother never got over her death. I think now, how strange it was that Marilyn's name was never mentioned in our house. Yet hers was the only picture that ever hung on the wall. School photos of my brothers and me were always put away. Could it be that mother forever cried all her tears away in her grief?

I bury my face in a tissue.

Oh, Lord, how can I deal with this? Help me to love Mother every second I have her. I glance at the clock on the wall, 11:00. The hospital floor is quiet this morning. The room is quiet, except for Mother's breathing.

I turn and look out the window toward the horizon, across the dark blue bay, to the barrier islands of Longport and Ocean City. The sun casts thousands of sparkles on the water. *Lord, the last place Mother and I went was to the far end of Longport. I can see the end of the island of Longport from here. We sat on the cement seawall at the beach, just off the jetty.*

"Just look at that water," Mom had said. She raised her arms like a maestro conducting his orchestra.

"It's really rough today," I said.

"I love the water, I always have. I am a water-baby," she said. Then she laughed, never taking her eyes off the mounting waves. "I'm drawn to it, whether it's a stream, a river, or the ocean." She tucked her hands into the pockets of her white wind breaker. "There is nothing like the sea, though." Her eyes looked out past the clanging buoy in the middle of the channel to a ship on the horizon. White water sprayed up against the blue sky as waves hurled themselves to the beach with a thundering sound.

Lord, I think of Your Psalm that says, "The Lord on high is mightier than the noise of many waters, than the mighty waves of the sea." Thank you for this beautiful beach. I look at my mother. *Lord, thank you for my mom, for her wisdom, her guidance, and her love for me.*

Sitting next to her on the seawall, I looked at her eyes behind the lenses of her glasses as she scanned the ocean. They were as blue as the sea itself. She looked down the wide length of beach. I followed her gaze; the beach was empty. No one was there. Nothing moved except the wind-blown rivulets of sugary sand along the water's edge, and the sea. But the sounds of the seashore—the birds, the waves, the wind, and breakers against the rocks—made the beach seem anything but empty. Mother's blonde hair blew in the wind, sticking straight up in the air, but I didn't tell her that. I smiled. I looked to my right; waves crashed over the shiny black rocks of the jetty, then washed back into the ocean. We sat on the seawall for a long time, not needing any more words.

*   *   *

Mother's been in the hospital for more than two weeks. This afternoon my brothers, Frankie, Ronnie, Scottie and Kennie, my Bill, and I are meeting with a palliative care specialist to discuss the rapid deterioration of Mother's health. We sit in a conference room on the fourth floor of the hospital. Even with the beautiful view outside the large windows, the room is somber.

"Margaret is very, very ill. Her major organs are starting to shut down," the doctor gently tells us. He is young and handsome. He looks us in the eyes and quietly tells us how the body starts to shut down and what we should expect.

"How long does she have left?" Scottie asks point blank.

"Well, if she stays in the hospital, we can keep her alive for a very long time. But she would be alive, and that's all," he says.

"Oh," I say. Bill squeezes my hand. I look at him and then at my brothers.

"She wouldn't want that," Ronnie says. "She told me she never wanted to be kept alive."

"Yes, she told me that too," I say.

Scottie, Kennie, and Frankie nod in agreement.

The doctor continues, "If you choose to put her on hospice care, she will live perhaps five days, no more."

*   *   *

The Ocean City 9th Street drawbridge is up. A tall-masted sailboat makes a starboard tack across the choppy bay towards the opened bridge. Traffic is heavy today because it's Saturday, and Memorial Day weekend. I'm not thinking at all of picnics or parades or the beach this holiday. I worry instead. *Lord, I pray that we did the right thing putting Mother in hospice care. I know she cannot go on like this. She's so frail and weak. Please give me some peace about this, Lord.*

The traffic along the bridge starts to move in both directions when the barricades swing to each side. I turn right at the first traffic light in town. The nursing home is only a mile down this road. *Lord, help me today. I really need it.*

People loaded with beach bags, chairs, and their children, cross the street at every corner on their way to the beach.

How can it be such a beautiful day when my mother is dying? I stop at a light, lean my fist against my chin, my elbow on the car door; I bite my lip and tears sting my eyes.

I park the car in the back parking lot of the nursing home and sit there for a minute. I lean my head against my hands on the steering wheel. I have to smile—smile for my mother. I cannot let her see me so upset.

I can't do this, Lord.

I hear laughing gulls squawking overhead. I look up and see blue sky, white puffy clouds, and trees blowing in the wind. *All of it is Your handiwork, Lord, Yours. Yes, Lord, I know You are with me.*

I enter the nursing home through glass doors, sign in at the front desk, and take the elevator to the fourth floor. I knock lightly on the door to Mother's room, peek in, and smile. Then I go into her new room.

Mother glares at me with wide-open eyes, tries to sit up, and shouts out loud: **"What'd you do? Bring me here to die?"** She clutches the edge of the blanket.

Lord, help me! What do I say?

I look at the floor. I can't look in her eyes. She turns her head away. I go and take her hand, but she yanks her hand away from mine. She hasn't talked in days, or even eaten solid food. She hasn't been out of bed or fed herself in almost a month.

"Hell-lo, Margaret!" a voice bellows from behind me as if on cue. I turn and see a nurse who fills up the entire door frame. Not only does she have a booming voice and a gigantic build, she has on a uniform that is bursting at the seams, and a head of bright yellow hair. She looks like a big,

German fräulein. She stands there with one hand on her hip and a clipboard in the other.

"**Why am I here**?" Mother shouts.

"Why, Margaret, you are very sick," the nurse says, raising her hands like a teacher proving a point.

"**I ... I am**?" Mother says in disbelief. She stares at the nurse for a moment, then at me. She sinks back on her pillow and turns her head away. It seems like all her strength went away too.

My brothers and I visit Mother for the next two days; she gets weaker and weaker. Our children come home to see their mom-mom. Mother goes into a coma on the third day.

That evening, about seven o'clock, Bill, Abbey, and I go to see her. She is breathing heavily and sporadically. Her head is turned slightly to her right on the pillow. I kiss her, brush her hair with my hand, and hold her tiny hand. Then I look at her face. I cannot believe what I see!

"Bill, look!" I say, "Abbey, look!"

I point to her left eye. In the corner of her eye is a tear. We all stare.

I settle on a chair next to her and hold her hand. Her hands are swollen. Her breathing is loud and raspy; it stops then starts again a few seconds later. I stare at the tear. I can't talk. No words get past my throat. But I know that God is with her and us; yes, He is here in this very room.

So, I hum hymns to her, low and soft, behind the mass in my throat. I hum the old-time hymns like "Ivory Palaces," "Trust and Obey," and "What a Friend We Have in Jesus." I remember hearing those songs in the first church we went to in Philadelphia, where my dad would give me pennies to put through the cracks of the old slatted wooden chairs to keep me quiet and occupied. But there I listened to the music.

The tear stays in the corner of Mother's eye. It never trickles down her cheek.

We leave Mother around eleven. I kiss her good-bye, then Bill does. Abbey comes out of Mother's room a few minutes later, crying. We hug each other and cry together, Abbey, Bill, and I, there in the hallway outside her room.

Abbey wipes her tears away and whispers to me, "Mommy, I told Mom-Mom I'd take care of you." We hug for a long time.

Mother died three hours later, at two in the morning. I would have stayed if I had known she would be gone so soon, but I didn't know. I regret that now, but I have a certainty in my heart that my mother would not have wanted me to see her last breath.

I find great comfort knowing that Mother is now with my father and Marilyn in heaven.

*   *   *

A few months later, a colleague of mine at the high school where I work tells me she has something she wants me to read. Her mother was just put in hospice care. A counselor gave her a pamphlet that chronicles the last days of life.

"I read this and I thought of you right away," my friend says.

The traumatic loss of my mother is still raw in my heart. I do not know if I want to read anything about death. I can't imagine what it is that she thinks is so important.

Then, I cannot believe what I read:

Now and then a tear gathers in one eye, or rolls down the cheek, minutes or hours before death, as if preparing us that death is approaching sooner than we think. This is 'the heralding tear' and it's a communication from the dying person to prepare their loved ones. Again, remaining open to possibility during this remarkable time will make it more likely that you won't miss some of these final gifts.

Thank you, Lord, for that final gift, a miracle gift, from my mother. She was telling me: "Good-bye, I love you. It's okay for me to go."

Lord, Your eye is on the sparrow.

The Way Home

*T*onight, I leave Rowan University early. My class is over. I turn up my collar against the blast of cold air as I leave the warmth of Westby Hall. The book bag weighs a ton on my shoulder, loaded with too many papers and books I did not use.

Briefly, I glimpse a tiny star against the black sky that lies beyond the amber glow of the lampposts; then the sky blackens again. I hold back the tears. I can go all week, all month, all year and be okay; but when I leave class, leave here, Rowan, there is a tightness in my throat. "Gosh, Mom," I scream inside my head, "*Why'd* **you have to die?**"

I scan the parking lot. No students are around. I am alone even now. The wind blows in my face like a smack of reality, "Grow up, kid," it seems to say. I bury my face in my scarf. I find my car, slide my key into the lock, lug my book bag across to the passenger seat, and climb in behind the wheel.

I miss the times, for years, I would leave class at night and go to Mom's house near this campus. She was my confidante, my encourager, my mentor, and my greatest fan. Her home was a haven of happiness. Driving down the hill of Abbington Lane, the only lamppost on the street beckons me to come in, have a cup of tea. It is Mom's lamppost. I pull the car in the driveway and the light of that clear bulb sort of winks at me—it twinkles—and it seems to say, "Glad you're here. Come on in!"

I reach the front door of Mom's house and the door opens. I see her there, smartly dressed in a red Christmas sweater, tan slacks, sheepskin slippers. She says, "Hi! What a great surprise!" even though I come every week. Then she fades away—evaporates into thin air. I am pulled backward across her walk, past the now dark lamppost to the seat of my car and a dark parking lot at Rowan. I cry, and cry hard, for a long time.

I start the car, turn off the noisy radio, and drive through the parking lot. I ease onto the street crowded with cars, Christmas shoppers, I guess. I want to drive past Mom's old house, but it is not the same. The white lamppost is still there, but there is no welcoming glow. The twinkle has been replaced by a cold fluorescent bulb. The house is usually dark, curtains drawn tight.

I turn my car away from Abbington Lane. Five minutes later, I am at the intersection of a four-lane highway that leads home. I stop at the traffic light.

In front of me, crossing the busy street, is a very young couple with three small children, ages five, four, and two years, maybe. They are dressed in warm clothes but are hurrying across the dark road at nine o'clock on a cold Wednesday night in December. I wonder where they are going. The young mother's face shows lines of worry as she carries the littlest child and shields her from the strong wind. They reach the corner where an Exxon gas station used to be. It is boarded up and dark. They step onto the curb. The light changes and I make a right-hand turn onto the busy pike.

I step on the gas. Then, breaking the silence in my car, a clear voice says: "Give them your money."

I know that voice. I have heard it before. It is God. When God speaks to me, I've learned to listen. But I zoom past the entrance of a strip mall where I could have turned around.

"Lord, how can I?" I ask. *"I'd have to go all the way back."* I keep my eyes on the flashing taillights in front of me. I brake, then speed up, keeping up with the heavy traffic.

Then again, an even louder voice says: "Give them your money."

"Lord, how would I know where they've gone?" I am driving fifty miles an hour down the pike. I'm already more than a mile away. I don't turn around.

Then, I hear a still, small voice, say: *"Do it unto Me."*

I move to the right-hand lane, turn right at the next light, swing into the parking lot of an automotive shop, and make a U-turn. I head back in the other direction. When I stop at the next traffic light, I grab my handbag and sift through receipts and papers in my wallet. I find a five-dollar bill and a twenty, no coins; it is all I have.

"This is nuts, Lord," I say as the light changes. *"How will I ever find them now?"* I pass stores, restaurants, and a crowded diner. I scan full parking lots for five people rushing home against the icy wind. I peer down side streets. I don't see them.

Finally, I return to the intersection where I last saw the small family. I pull into the left-turn lane and stop at the traffic light. I look over at the old gas station. My eyes adjust from the glare of oncoming headlights to the darkness of the corner. There they are, the five of them, huddled in the shelter of a small glass-enclosed bus stop.

The mother sits on the bench facing me, holding her little girl. She doesn't smile; she looks at the ground. The two boys hop around in the booth. The father stands and talks to his wife with his hands in his jacket pockets.

The traffic light shows a green left arrow. I turn. I drive another thirty feet and make another quick left and turn into the abandoned gas station. I slow down and pull to the front of the station. I stop my car twenty feet behind the bus stop booth. The father looks up, his clear eyes wonder. As I roll the window down, he looks me in the eye and smiles. I motion him toward me with my red gloved finger.

"You all right, lady?" he says with concern in his voice as he walks toward my car.

I laugh. "Yes, I'm fine."

He laughs, too. Even in the dim light I can tell his hazel eyes have a lot of green in them, and a sort of mysterious kindness. He is very young and has dark curly hair like a young Rocky Balboa. He is not very tall; his eyes are level with mine—he is standing, I'm in my SUV.

I slide my left arm out the window with the money folded in half between my thumb and index finger. I cannot help but smile. I have no words.

"What's this?" he asks. His eyebrows raise and the green flecks in his eyes act like question marks.

"The Lord told me to give this to you," I say quietly.

"He did? Really?"

"Yes, He did; and when He speaks, I've learned to listen."

We look at each other. The only thing that connects us at this moment is wonder. I feel it and he shows it.

"You and your family have a merry Christmas," I say.

"You have a merry Christmas, too." He looks at me and then the gift. "Thank you," he quietly says. He turns back to his family.

I pull forward to the driveway exit of the gas station and wait for some cars to pass. The station doesn't seem so dark and abandoned now. I turn onto the pike; it is as if the ground is not below my tires. I leave the small family and begin my hour-long journey home to Somers Point.

I hear no voices as I travel the same route I did twenty minutes ago. I feel a warmth spread from my heart to my head to my toes. Christmas lights rush by with the miles. I stop and go at traffic lights not thinking of my driving, but of the Christmas family. I smile and ask myself; did that really happen? Maybe I helped the couple when they needed it. Maybe they doubted what Christmas was all about.

Then, it struck me. I should have taken them to their house! Instead, I left them in the cold night waiting for a bus. I never thought of getting them home. How could I have left them there?

The lonely dark highway is lit only by my bright headlights. The yellow dotted line dividing the lanes swishes by in a blur. My mind recalls the face of the young father: the clean-shaven round face with clear alabaster skin, the gentle smile, his eyes full of kindness, and that curly dark brown hair blowing in the night wind. He asked me if *I* was all right. And then there was the wonder. Yes, it is the wonder I think about most.

Then, I know.

It was not *I* who helped this father; it was *he* who helped *me*. That young father was an angel sent to help me. The wonder, the eyes, the mysterious kindness were all part of God's gift to me. The blanket of love I feel wrapped in is heaven sent; it is like a mother's hug. Yes, that is it, a mother's hug. It's just what I needed!

On the winding back road close to home, Christmas lights outline trees and houses. The night is moonless. A manger scene is lit up on a front lawn, a shepherd is blown over in the wind; Joseph looks at mother and child. My thoughts drift to that young father, also traveling late at night with his family—not stopping at a bus stop, but at a stable. I wonder, did the innkeeper know the gift he was given?

I turn onto our street and see the welcoming light of my home at the far end of the street. I realize now the angel did not need my money. God had to see if I would give all I had to Him. I also now know why God didn't tell me to give them a ride home. Angels can get wherever they are going pretty fast without me.

I swing into my driveway and turn off the car. The porch light, that clear bulb, sort of winks at me—it twinkles—and it says, "Glad you're here. Come on in."

Acknowledgements

I would not have been able to write *Apples of Gold in Settings of Silver* without the help of so many people in my life. I am so thankful for their guidance and love throughout this writing process.

To my professors at Rowan University, thank you. I have studied with the finest in the field of writing. I thank each of you for your dedication, guidance, and your words of wisdom to me.

Thank you, Bob McCormick, my friend, and the man who first encouraged me to put my stories together, so others could enjoy them. You were the one who read my very first draft. Your keen sense of the written word has taught me more about the power of our words.

To all my 'readers,' the friends and family who read this manuscript before it was sent to press. Your love, feedback, and encouragement have given me great hope.

Thank you, Geoff Affleck, for the direction you have given me along this journey. I could not have done it without your knowledge and help. You directed me every step of the way from leading me to a wonderful editor to seeing this book in print. You are truly a master of your craft.

Thank you, Marial Shea, my editor. You have been the north star of this writing process. Your literary knowledge, careful and precise editing, and guidance made my words flow together with power and grace.

My family is my universe and without them these stories could not have been told. Thank you, Wendy, Greg, Gavin, Abbey, and Cami for your love and for being the greatest children in the world. Thank you for the comical antics and frustrating challenges you gave Dad and me when you were growing up. As each of you matured, I have witnessed your integrity, your dedication to achieve your goals, your zest for life, and your faithful spirit. You have inspired me to work hard to complete this collection of stories.

Most of all, thank you, Bill, my husband, and my best friend, for believing in me. Thank you for telling me, "You can do it," when I did not have the words. Thank you for the cups of tea you brought me late at night when I was writing. When God gave me you, He gave me the absolute best. Your unconditional love, your strength, and your faith have made me into the woman I am today. I love you with all my heart.

About the Author

*D*eborah Louise Off is a wife, mother of five, and proud grandmother of eight. She earned her Bachelor of Arts and Master of Writing degrees from Rowan University after twenty years of traveling to night classes. Now a high school substitute teacher, she also serves on the editorial board of Philadelphia Stories Magazine and is a former adjunct professor. Deborah loves traveling with her husband, Bill, especially to the national parks of the United States and Canada. At home, she enjoys playing the piano and writing short stories that celebrate the wonders in everyday life.